FEARLESS
FINANCES

CASSANDRA CUMMINGS

FEARLESS FINANCES

A Timeless Guide to Building Wealth

HarperCollins
Leadership

An Imprint of HarperCollins

Learn more and download resources at
http://thefearlessfinances.com.

Published by HarperCollins Leadership, an imprint of HarperCollins Focus LLC.

Any internet addresses, phone numbers, or company or product information printed in this book are offered as a resource and are not intended in any way to be or to imply an endorsement by HarperCollins Leadership, nor does HarperCollins Leadership vouch for the existence, content, or services of these sites, phone numbers, companies, or products beyond the life of this book.

ISBN 978-1-4002-3040-2 (eBook)
ISBN 978-1-4002-3038-9 (HC)

Library of Congress Control Number: 2022935498

Printed in the United States of America
22 23 24 25 26 LSC 10 9 8 7 6 5 4 3 2 1

DISCLAIMER

Investing in securities involves risks, and there is always the potential of losing money when you invest in securities. Cassandra Cummings and affiliates do not provide legal, tax, or accounting advice. You should review any planned financial transactions that may have tax or legal implications with your personal tax or legal advisor.

Before investing, consider carefully the investment objectives, risks, charges, and expenses of the security, including management fees, other expenses, and special risks. This and other information may be found in each fund's prospectus or summary prospectus, if available. Always read the prospectus or summary prospectus carefully before you invest or send money.

This material is not intended as a recommendation, offer, or solicitation for the purchase or sale of any security or investment strategy.

Investment and insurance products:

- Are not FDIC insured
- Are not bank guaranteed
- May lose value
- Are not deposits
- Are not insured by any federal government agency
- Are not a condition to any banking service or activity

The author and the publisher assume no responsibility for any injuries suffered or damages incurred during or as a result of the use or application of the information contained herein.

This book is dedicated to my favorite girl and daughter, Nia. May you continue to be fearless when it comes to whatever your heart desires.

CONTENTS

INTRODUCTION

I had typed my resignation letter at least a month prior. I looked at it the night before meeting with my director at Merrill, adding and deleting words, trying to strike the right tone.

I went back and forth, moving my eyes across the screen, reciting the words in my head to be sure it was professional and that I was clear and firm, but not "angry" as so many Black women who express themselves are perceived. I sat in fear, but I hit the blue "send" button and gasped for air, proud of myself for finally going through with it.

The next morning, I sat across from my director. He was an African American man who had risen fairly quickly within the firm. We had a brief discussion about me staying on, but I knew in my heart that my time at the firm had run its course. I had been a financial advisor to thousands of affluent individuals and families over the span of fifteen years. I witnessed accounts flourish and investors hit new tax brackets, with the help of my advice and guidance. I received holiday cards and delicious treats in gratitude for the financial impact that I had imparted on their lives for generations to come. But, for the longest time, I felt a void.

I've come a long way. I used to be a little girl growing up on welfare who saw my mother clutch every dollar so tightly. It created a fear so deep down that it would take decades to build the courage to view money in a different way. Today, I am a woman who stared down my financial fears, built lasting connections, and turned my passion for finances into a business where I could do what I love in the way I love to do it: as an entrepreneur.

I'm Cassandra Cummings, the oldest of six sisters, a mother, a daughter, and the fearless founder of The Stocks & Stilettos Society, a community of women at various stages of their investing journey.

I want you to keep in mind that no mistakes are made in this game called life, starting with the hand that I was dealt. I was once ashamed of my beginnings, with a teenage mother who was illiterate and a father who lost his life after "tapping the streets" (to put it politely) to provide for his family and his community. Now that I'm over the embarrassment, it has allowed me to kick down doors to limiting beliefs about money and to show others how to do the same, while creating generational wealth—starting with me.

A great irony that loomed over me like a dark cloud was that I was highly educated, successful in my career, but financially illiterate. At the time, I couldn't put my finger on why I was having such a hard time financially. I did everything I was told to do—I went to school, got good grades, and got a good job. I had solid credit and a small, but decent, savings account. But something wasn't adding up.

THE STOCKS & STILETTOS SOCIETY

I wanted to help more women that looked like me to close the race, gender, and investment gaps—or straight up, the economic gap. The statistics were becoming increasingly startling. I knew that so many women were trying to break generational and financial curses and trying to learn how money works, just as I was, but had no one to guide them. They were on their own, trying to figure it out, and making costly mistakes. Or even worse, they weren't doing anything at all besides tucking their money away in a savings account. Therefore, I created The Stocks & Stilettos Society, an online community of over one hundred thousand women investors, as a safe space for women to have a place to ask questions and learn about investing in the stock market. We talk about money and investing like some groups talk about parenting and relationships. It's different. It works.

The Society has become the largest community of Black women investors to ever assemble. It's a sisterhood—a financial sorority, if you will. It's unlike any other organization I've been a part of—we truly help each other to win, financially. And to think that *I*, a young Black woman from Oakland, California with so many disadvantages, created this powerful investing community!

WHO IS THIS BOOK FOR?

This book is not a traditional "get rich quick" or "money advice" guide, because my path was anything but those things. In *Fearless Finances* you're not going to hear vague, unhelpful tips like these:

- Pay yourself first.
- Save for a rainy day.
- Invest in your 401(k) to get the match.

We'll talk about savings, investments, and retirement strategies, but in addition to some tried-and-true ways, I'll also present a number of options you may not have considered.

Fearless Finances may help someone just starting out on her financial journey. This book is also for the sister who has been a good steward of her money. See if any of the following statements apply to you:

- You are a budgeting queen.
- You have conquered the journey to good credit.

- You may have a small side hustle, but you want to know how you can put a stop to your money hustling backward.
- You know how to save and invest, but you're asking yourself, "What's next?"

In that last question—"What's next?"—I heard hope for the future. But I also heard a lot of fear, from one group in particular.

THE SIDELINE SISTERS

Many women have a hard time articulating what they want when it comes to money. They might say, "I want a million dollars." But that doesn't mean they know if it's really enough for their future needs, or what it takes to amass that amount.

I've also heard women say over and over again, "My husband takes care of the finances." This makes me cringe and give my sister the death stare. I have had several clients sit across from me, full of emotion, as they attempt to manage their finances after a divorce or death. Trust me, the clients who've had an "awakening" with their money are the most challenging. The challenges aren't just about inheriting a lump sum such as a life insurance policy. There's also an onslaught of new information and skills that must be activated in either a sudden crisis like the death of a spouse, or a slow-moving crisis like a divorce. (Even in the best of cases, divorces have a way of chewing up time, emotions, and money.) The mindset shift that immediately needs to be adopted can prove daunting. These clients have to adjust from "He has always taken care of _____" to "I am now taking care of _____." You have to be ready—even if you don't think you can or want to be.

These "sideline sisters," as I like to call them, are women who have the capital and the flexibility to make sound, rewarding investments. But because they're afraid of changing their ideas around money, they keep it parked, or "sidelined," in investment vehicles that are safe with the least amount of risk. You may be asking, "Why on earth would *anyone* do that?!" It's more common than you think. In fact, you might be one of these women right now. Perhaps someone else like a husband or partner handles the money in your household. Maybe you are so excited that after so many years of grinding, you have discretionary funds in your account, and that, in and of itself, feels like enough. Again, if you are a first-generation wealth builder like myself (and so many women of color and Black women, in particular), there is a temptation to pat yourself on the back for getting as far as you have. But I am here to tell you that this is not enough. You may be the sister who listens to her friends talk about their money moves. The irony of the sideline sister is that she watches the market, cheers her sisters as they win with money, but she may be stuck in six-figure land or doesn't think she is worthy of winning financially when it comes to her personal wealth.

WHY SHOULD YOU BE FEARLESS
WITH YOUR FINANCES?

According to an April 2019 article in the *Washington Post*, women own 32 cents to every dollar owned by men and the average woman's net worth is just $5,541.[1] For women of color, these figures are even lower. *Fearless Finances* will help women to close this wealth gap. I want you to hold in your hands a book that will give you the courage to face your fears about money. Not only will the information in this book lead you to sound financial tips, beginning investment instruction, and intergenerational wealth strategies, it will provide you with so much more. The bottom line is that this book will give you three things: clarity, confidence, and control.

You'll gain *clarity* by seeing money in a new way and by thinking about it with fresh inspiration. You'll be able to see investing as a long-term strategy with many different options that fit your personality, available time, and interests.

You'll gain *confidence* because you will have resources at your fingertips. You won't have to stumble around in the proverbial dark, "doing research on the internet" looking for help or ideas. I am your personal guide to the terrain of investing.

Finally, you'll get *control* of your finances by letting go of your tight control of money and allowing it to flow freely and abundantly in the right direction.

I want to help more women like you, who seek to dream in color, to gain control over their finances, and to pick up the confidence it takes to catch these coins. I want this book to help my daughter and all of my sisters to never be fearful about money again.

As the saying goes, scared money doesn't make money. As women, we have a different set of priorities than men, and often those priorities take time away from other important things such as our money. Investing, and all of its unknowns, can keep us fearful and out of the game. By the time we have checked the boxes on all of the other items on our list, there are only seconds left on the clock. That leaves us scrambling to play catch-up at the last minute and somehow learn how to multiply money. Women who are tardy to the party come into the group with these questions, repeatedly:

- Where do I start?
- How would you invest $1,000 or $10,000?
- I have no idea what to do. Can somebody help me?
- How much do I need to start investing?
- How many shares should I buy?

This book will help you get in the game, put on a full-court press with your money, and have you walking out a true champion, as a first-generation wealth builder.

A WEALTH SHIFT IS UPON US

At the onset of the global pandemic of 2020, many lost their jobs. For others, the shelter-in-place orders gave them the permission they needed to think differently about their money and creating wealth. Such a radical and forced shift across the world caused many of us to adopt a new normal on how we live our lives and finance our futures. The stock market became the go-to for replacing income and the makings of creating wealth.

Some experts would argue that education is the great equalizer. But I beg to differ. Managing your money, growing your investments, and protecting your wealth can level the playing field—no matter your background or education level—more than what any formal training can do.

Money touches everyone. Its impact can be far-reaching if you have it, and it can make your life a living hell if you lack enough of it (which is all relative, right?).

The money industry has made trillions by using many Americans as financial prey, which is why many of our schools avoid teaching us how to get "it"—financial security. Personal finance, investing, and retirement are often lifelong lessons that are learned through on-the-job experience. But this method can be costly—as many Americans have had to learn the hard way.

It took nearly a half-century for me to become financially solvent—and then a millionaire. I want to give you the guide, the blueprint, to wealth in an effort to avoid the pitfalls I encountered, simply because I had to learn through trial and error.

But what if you had someone like the person on the tarmac at the airport, sporting a reflective vest with those handheld orange sticks, directing you to the runway of wealth? Would you be less fearful to turn right? Would you gain confidence in moving forward? Ultimately, would you behave better when it comes to your money?

This is why I wrote this book, now.

IN EACH SECTION I will guide you through the investment process by first defining important terms and then outlining what they look like in real life. Then, I will present to you different options and strategies to make your money work for you.

Fearless Finances isn't a read-it-and-set-it-down type of book. I am going to ask you to do some work on behalf of yourself. I will share what I call "Money Moves." These tips are designed to help you with the most important part of investing. I have done them myself and they work. Do you have your "Success Squad" in place? Not to worry, each chapter offers one of the greatest success hacks: getting the right people around you. With the "Success Squad" sections, I'll help you identify and enlist people who can help you level up. Also, throughout the book, I have included stories of "Fearless Figures"—women just like you who have forged their own paths to financial success. I hope they will encourage you to do the same.

Let's do this.

PART 1

Fearless Footprint
Survival

Money management can be challenging and costly when you are simply trying to make it to the next day. Living paycheck to paycheck is no fun, and in this section, the goal is to give you tools that you can use for the foundational areas of personal finance. Once your survival needs have been more or less satisfied, then you can keep driving toward your next level.

ONE

Mind Right, Money Ready

Your mind will believe whatever you tell it.
Tell yourself you're fearless and do it scared.

"Why aren't you rich?" This question was posed to me when I attended a business event and I was looking to grow my business. It was a very interesting question because I had all of the makings of becoming rich, but there was something obviously not connecting to get me to the next level. What I came to realize is that it was my mindset. Growing up in the projects and living in lack had me believing that I wasn't worthy of becoming wealthy. But positioning myself and being around women who looked like me but who were six- and seven-figure earners began to transform my thinking about becoming wealthy. These dope women had many things in common, but one characteristic stood out: they were *fearless*. Many Black women have been programmed or conditioned to think that it's all about working harder.

At the end of the day, it comes down to mindset. It's not necessarily the hard part, but the smart part. We have to do the work, but typically we're not rich because of our mindset. There are some barriers, such as systemic racism, which I will discuss in a later chapter, that can hinder us from becoming rich. But what we can control is our mindset. We have to understand that first comes the mindset, then comes the money.

WHEN YOUR MIND CHANGES, YOUR EXPECTATIONS CHANGE

"The first step toward getting somewhere is deciding you're not going to stay where you are." That was said by the late Alison "CiCi" Gunn, who was affectionately known as the "Six Figure Chick." I remember when I first started creating and posting financial content on social media, I came across this young Black woman who was showing people how to increase their social media presence. She had a very particular mindset that she was going to make a certain amount of money for the week, for the day, for that hour, and so on. She was very specific about her goals and how she was going to reach them. CiCi was very transparent about how she was going to execute her strategy.

I loved reading her posts and watching her videos. She broke down the specifics of her exact plans to achieve certain follower goals, as well as certain monetary goals. One of her favorite sayings was, "Who got my money?" The boisterous way in which she belted it out into the camera always tickled me. It really gave me the idea of shifting how I thought about obtaining wealth. With billions of people on the planet, there are plenty of people to buy and sell to. The root of the word *affluent* means "to flow," which means there is plenty of money to go around—there's enough for everyone.

Learning from CiCi made me realize something else: you have to be the best thing that ever happened to your money. Bottom line, no one is going to take care of your money the way that you're going to take care of it. When you come to these realizations and you truly begin to take ownership of your financial success, it really starts to shift your thinking on how you should proceed toward achieving your financial objectives.

> You have to be the best thing that
>
> ever happened to your money.

First of all, you have to be honest with yourself about wanting financial independence: doing what you want, whenever you want, and with the people you want. We typically equate more money with either happiness or control over our own lives. That's really why we want to have more money.

Black women have been earning degrees at a higher rate than any other group of women in the US since 2015–2016.[1] I recall looking in the mirror and saying to myself, "You are too smart and too pretty to be this broke." I remember saying this to myself in spite of my years in school, plus my degrees and certifications. I just couldn't figure out why I wasn't where I wanted to be financially. I had my health, my family, and a good job, but something wasn't adding up. Not even my professional network, which was growing, could help me figure out why I wasn't rich.

HEY, I GET IT. You don't know what you don't know, including an abundant and wealthy mindset. To adopt such a mindset, you need to see it. You have to raise your standards around the people who you surround yourself with and get around successful people. They think differently. They move differently. They make money work for them. Hang around positive, financially successful people because you will more than likely begin to think like them.

Depending on what their dominant thoughts are, they could help you or hold you back.

> Surround yourself with those that will only
> lift you higher. —Oprah Winfrey

My friends in high school thought differently than my friends in college. Different people, different geography, different life experiences. These factors, among others, influenced my thoughts. When I was in college, I was surrounded by people whose goals were different from mine, but what we had in common was that, wherever we were starting from, we wanted to get to the next level. We didn't all want to work at the same firm, but we knew we had to sharpen our skill sets. We leaned on each other for advice and observed each other's actions, looking for (and often imitating) behaviors that would inspire us and push us to our desired next level. Which brings me to the next point.

WHEN YOUR EXPECTATIONS CHANGE, YOUR BEHAVIOR CHANGES

When you set the expectation to be rich, your behavior moves in that direction. What if you've never been in the presence of a rich person? What if you don't know any millionaires? Well, it will require you to step outside of your comfort zone and push yourself to meet and observe new people. In this case, you have to tell your mind that fear is not an option.

Carol Dweck, a psychology professor at Stanford University, states, "The passion for stretching yourself and sticking to it, even (or especially) when it's not going well, is the hallmark of the growth mindset. This is the mindset that allows people to thrive during some of the most challenging times in their lives."[2] If I set my intention to earn a million dollars, that's definitely going to allow my behavior to shift; it puts me in the frame of mind to earn a million dollars. What does that look like? For me, it was studying the habits of people who were millionaires.

I'm going to look at different things that people can do, or people have done, to make a million dollars. I'm going to have conversations with people who have made a million dollars because now I've elevated my expectations. That alone challenges my thinking. My behavior was realigned to actually move in that direction. So I'm now taking in different data sets, different amounts of knowledge, that are specifically focused on how to make a move in that direction.

An important question to ask yourself is the same question I asked myself at the beginning of my journey: "Do I want to be a millionaire, or do I want a million dollars?" These are two distinctly different ideas because you can be a millionaire and have financial resources worth a million or more, or you can have access to a million dollars to spend.

Let's break this down.

You can be a millionaire in terms of your assets, both liquid and illiquid. *Liquid* means you can spend it right away. *Illiquid* (or not liquid) means you don't have immediate access; you must convert the asset to cash.

You have to understand that once you spend money, it's not coming back. If you spend a dollar, that ends the dollar—it doesn't come back to you. It's okay to want to have a million dollars to spend, but you have to first build up to that amount of money. We'll look at how you can overcome the fear and adopt the mindset that you are deserving and willing to do the work required to either be a millionaire, or have a million dollars to spend. That's going to bring me to my third point.

MONEY, POWER, AND DISRESPECT

For generations, the formula we've been sold is to go to school, get good grades, and get a great job. In part that is a road map to financial success. But there is so much that has been left out of that equation. Wealth building is equal parts discipline and planning. Those parts are up to you and are mostly under your control. But I would be remiss if I didn't call attention to a factor that can disrupt even our best-laid financial plans, if we let it—racial discrimination. That factor is the part that you can't see but might be more impactful than all of your planning.

Over a hundred years ago, "Black Wall Street" in the Greenwood neighborhood of Tulsa, Oklahoma, was a burgeoning community of over six hundred Black-owned businesses. It was destroyed by a racist mob within a twenty-four-hour span back in 1921. Generations of hard work and Black wealth were destroyed, never to recover.

But we don't have to go back a hundred years to tell the story of financial malfeasance. Consider Marin County, California, or Indianapolis, Indiana.[3] Both cities were in the news at the end of 2021 for what Black homeowners call "whitewashing" their homes in order to get more favorable appraisals. The "appraisal gap" is the difference between what a home is worth versus its value based on a number of factors. But when a homeowner is Black, they are more likely to have the appraised value of the home diminished, reducing the amount of money they can make from the sale. In Indianapolis, the home's original appraisal was less than half its actual market value. In Marin County, the home was appraised *a half-million dollars* less than it should have been.

Across the country, homes in Black and Latino neighborhoods were more likely to be appraised below the contract price compared to white neighborhoods (12.5 percent and 15.4 percent versus 7.4 percent, respectively).[4]

Wealth theft can be unseen, an ominous force that generational wealth builders continually have to push against at nearly every turn. When it rears its ugly head, it may look like an appraisal gap or not being allowed to purchase an expensive handbag in a luxury retailer, not being allowed to purchase a major sports team, or be hired to coach one, despite years of experience and being highly qualified. It could also look like paying more in taxes as a single, Black woman than her white counterpart.[5] It can be as simple as being mistaken for the help at an upscale, charity dinner. It is almost always your intuition tugging on your emotions, an encounter or transaction that is unsettling in your spirit. Something is clearly out of alignment, despite following protocols and doing the right thing. You may say to yourself, "The math is not *mathing*."

To take a page out of *Who Moved My Cheese?* by Spencer Johnson, you not only have to anticipate, acknowledge, and accept change, but as Black women building wealth, we will also need to take it one step further and attack the problem head-on. It takes a village to raise a child, and we need to keep that same energy when it comes to our finances. It takes a village to build wealth. Lean on your Success Squad, as I have highlighted in each chapter of this book.

Education isn't enough because, if it were, Black women wouldn't be some of the most educated women with some of the least wealth.[6]

So, anticipate that the playing field will not be level, acknowledge that the goal line will be moved, accept that you will have to be ten times better, and attack each unnerving situation by calling on your village. In the words of the late Shirley Chisholm, "If they don't give you a seat at the table, bring a folding chair." I say, build your own table. Your heirs are counting on you to continue to rewrite and make history. You owe it to yourself to be *fearless*.

WHEN YOUR BEHAVIOR CHANGES, YOUR MONEY WILL FALL INTO PLACE

Here's a different but related example. You are trying to lose fifteen pounds. For weeks (or months, or maybe even years) you have gone about trying to lose those pounds through diet and exercise. But at some point, you get to the place where you realize, *My little workout video is not cutting it. I am going to try something different because I've got my mind made up that I want to lose these fifteen pounds. So now I expect to not let myself down. Therefore, I'm going to go find a trainer who is going to help me get on a plan.*

It's a new experience for you. Your trainer introduces you to a workout schedule. She gives you a realistic eating plan. She coaches you on how to remove the mental blocks that are keeping you from losing the fifteen pounds you have been struggling with—and it works. Now you are saying to yourself, "I am looking much cuter, I am happier, and I am healthier."

In short: small, consistent changes add up to a big change in behavior that starts to put things into place, including your finances. When practiced with focus and clear intent, this will obviously work for the better. Your trainer will provide you with the necessary information and tools. But only you can decide that you will implement that information and use the tools to achieve your desired results.

Fearless Finances works the same way. I am going to give you the information and tools to build the wealth that you have saved and turn it into the larger investment tool you desire. How quickly you implement these strategies is up to you.

As we begin, ask yourself, "Do I have to work for the next twenty years to get the money that I desire? Or could that be shortened significantly if I implement what is in this book? Can I cut my timeline down by seven years, ten years, or possibly more?"

It's very possible because money loves speed. Money comes to those who actually put things in motion. Once you start to move, once your behavior changes, once you start to actually do the things that are required to get you to the goal, you'll find that things will start to move into place.

A note about myself: I am a first-generation wealth builder. While money did flow in and out of my home because my father worked the streets of Oakland, I did not experience financial stability. There were times when we were flush with cash, and times when there was barely enough to keep the lights on. My father did the best he could. I inherited his love of the "coin" and his spirit of entrepreneurship, but I did not learn how to build my wealth. I wasn't afraid of money, but I was afraid to use it in a way that would be long term. You, too, might be a first-generation wealth builder. You might be doing pretty well compared to your family members or the people you grew up with. Now, while we love our family members and the people we grew up with, the reality is many of them are just not equipped to help us with the wealth-building tools that are necessary to change not only our lives, but the lives of people we care about. We have to surround ourselves with people who know more than us, who have demonstrated success with their money. We have to read books—like this one—to influence our behavior.

This brings me back to our mindset shift. As the first-generation wealth builders in our families, we are influential because there are loved ones watching what we do, including how we spend money. And so, as we work toward being the first-generation wealth builders in our families, we have to be eager to earn, and less willing to burn. Let me break this down for you. If you want your money to make money, then you will need to discipline yourself. You will need to resist the urge to spend money right away and cultivate the habit of allowing your money to sit tight until you have a bigger—and more lasting—purchases, like stocks and securities. It is tempting to spend money as soon as you have earned it. I know. I have experienced financial scarcity and insecurity so when I see a purse, a pair of shoes, or get an invitation for an expensive trip or dinner out, it is tempting to immediately say *yes*. We don't want to deny ourselves the item or experience that we know we deserve. But what I am saying is that six months, twelve months, or even four years from now is not a lot of time in comparison to the results you will yield when you develop the discipline to focus on *earning* rather than *burning* the money you have worked so hard to develop.

I remember attending an event in Los Angeles by Rachel Rodgers. It was called the "Million Dollar Badass" event. I was sitting in my seat with a few dozen ladies, taking copious notes. Rachel was saying a lot, but what stopped me in my tracks was her strategy to get to $5 million. Honestly, I hadn't even thought that far. I was thinking, "Six figures—can I get to six figures? I'd be happy." She just casually floated the notion of, "Let's get to the first million en route to the five million." I surveyed the room and I thought to myself, "Am I in the right room?" Because I was looking to make only six figures, but these women were obviously trying to get to the seven-figure mark and beyond. The lesson? The ability to be in the right room changed my expectations of myself. As a result, it also started to change my behavior. I left the event with a different expectation, which then changed my behavior, which ultimately put me in the position to make seven figures.

So, in this book, what I want to do is give you some things that you can use to change your mind. We'll go back to the heading of the first section in this chapter: when your mind changes, your expectations change. Shortly before Rachel Rodgers's event, I started writing and reciting affirmations for myself that boosted my mood in the morning and prepared me for the day. I believe it led me to her event. Even though I was surprised to learn what I was hearing, there I was in the room, with the mindset that I was a skilled, knowledgeable person who was capable of making unlimited amounts of money. I was ready to start with the first million.

THREE AFFIRMATIONS FOR AFFLUENCE

My first tip is to write down affirmations for yourself. To be honest, at first, I was never really big on affirmations. It felt a little awkward saying positive messages to myself morning after morning, but they worked. And what's more, in a way, we are constantly affirming messages to ourselves that aren't always positive. How many times have you said to yourself that you "can't save money" or money "always burns a hole through your pocket"? Or even worse: "You know I stay broke!"

Stop it!

Remember, it's a mindset. Like most things in life we want to master, we have to practice, repeat, and practice again. Once these affirmations take root—and they will if you practice daily—your mind shifts to a different set of expectations.

So here is my first Money Move affirmation:

I make unlimited sums of money with grace, and in a perfect way.

I tell myself to also keep in mind that I don't place a limit on what I can earn. I don't go into a project, a job, or anything of that nature, having a cap on what I'm able to earn or attract quickly. Remember, money loves speed. So, once I learn new information, I'm going to implement what I've learned in an expeditious way. Now, don't think the word *expeditiously* only means "fast" and "without thought or care." It also means efficient, meaning to achieve the best result with no wasted effort. It takes careful thought to do something in an elegant manner with no extra steps.

To *expedite* means to make a process happen soon. When I use the word *grace*, I mean with concern and thought. Putting these two ideas together creates a form of synergy. When we learn something new, we are typically excited and ready to implement what we have learned. What we must remember to do is use a measure of thought and care so that what we set out to do has the maximum potential for success.

My second Money Move affirmation is:

I clearly communicate my financial vision to myself and to others. I teach and I inspire.

Long before I became a financial and investment advisor, I was a math teacher. I have always loved numbers. One of the reasons The Stock & Stilettos Society has been successful is that the women in the group clearly communicate their financial desires. By doing so, they are able to inspire others to pitch in and help them get from point A to point B. It's a very interesting type of financial sorority, where women empower other women to accelerate their financial objectives by listening to their desires and providing them with the tools, necessary steps, and strategies to get there by way of the stock market.

My third and final Money Move affirmation is:

I radiate love and care toward myself and others.

You might be asking yourself, "What do love and care toward yourself, let alone others, have to do with money?" My answer: everything! Money has *a lot* of emotional weight, and it is one of the reasons we either spend too much or don't spend enough in the right places. It's the feeling of having saved $15,000 in a high-yield savings account with an above-industry average interest rate versus parking your money in a low-yield savings account with an interest rate barely above zero. It's the feeling of investing money in companies you care about and seeing those healthy quarterly dividend checks deposited into your account. It's the feeling of seeing a piece of property for sale and deciding to buy it, knowing that you can afford it. You get the idea. But you can't get to that place until you feel good about yourself and what you are capable of. Once you show love and kindness to yourself, you will reflect that in all of your choices including, *especially*, money. Remember, your money is working for you and through you. Be kind to yourself. Watch your money be kind right back.

COMMON FEARS ABOUT MONEY AND HOW TO OVERCOME THEM

Interestingly, 61 percent of women would rather talk about their own deaths than about money, according to a report by Merrill Lynch and Age Wave.[7] What this sobering statistic tells me is that as women we have to change our conversation to change our compensation. We have so many things that are working against us. We have the fact that we are usually the primary caregivers in our families. Women tend to take off work to care for children or elderly parents, which takes us out of the workforce. On average, we work about twenty-seven years compared to forty years for men. In effect, thirteen years less than the average definitely reduces our earning potential over time. We've got to be smarter about our money. And just in case you are still not convinced, women outlive their spouses or significant others by an average of five years. Those additional years will also need to be financed.

Now for some really sobering news. (I am sorry to give you this news, but this book is called *Fearless Finances,* and that includes facing statistics and obstacles that can be very scary.) Here goes: for every dollar a white man earns, a Black woman earns just 63 cents. In addition to all of the other gaps we face, we have a wage gap as well. With so many things working against us, we have to be smarter with our money and do what is often different and difficult. The first step is changing our mindset, which then helps us make different choices. The first step in doing something with our money is changing how we're conditioned around money.

But take heart. Our net worth is not tied to our net birth. We have to believe that where we were born, or who we were born to, is not a deciding factor in what our future will look like. If you have a higher *self-worth,* then you can achieve a higher *net worth* for you and your family. You will have to condition your mind to create substantial wealth. It won't be easy, but the mind is your most powerful asset.

Very often we don't do what is necessary to get to the next level because of fear. But it's a paradox: your fear of losing money is keeping you from your ability to actually grow your money. When we fear not having enough money or not knowing what to do with the money we have, we put off important decisions until we are forced to make a change. We are more likely to defer important decisions until something bad happens or an unforeseen emergency hits, and by that time, it's usually too late. In some cases, we deflect and defer our decisions around money by leaning on others to manage our finances for us. We can no longer afford to do that as women.

> You will have to condition your mind
>
> to create substantial wealth.

As women, we tend to be embarrassed that we don't understand finances better. It makes sense, too. Turn on the television or listen to a news program, and the financial experts are usually men. Where are the women speaking as financial authorities? We might think finances aren't for us because we don't *see us.* This is why it is important to become a part of communities in which talking about money is an accepted practice. Women need a safe space to talk about money issues. Consider this book your safe space, your financial community.

We have been conditioned to think that talking about money and finances is somehow dirty and rude. We are trained to believe that there is something impolite about wanting money and talking about wanting money. There is a lot of negative self-talk around finances, and that has to stop. Remember the affirmations I spoke about? This is one of the reasons you need them. You have to stop telling yourself that you don't deserve to have a lot of money, or you can't have prosperity. When you shift how you think and talk about yourself, you believe that you are worthy of having more money and will behave accordingly.

One last thing before we dive in: women are conditioned to be perfectionists in all aspects of our lives. Finances are no different. But investing and having money is not a straight line. It's not perfect. There was a review of Warren Buffett's portfolio which noted that out of 400 to 500 stocks, only ten were the ones that made the most money for him. The other 390 to 490 stocks were not perfect.

When it comes to money, you don't always have to be perfect. You just have to get it right more times than you get it wrong, and there is a strategy for that.

What does the next level look like? Once you increase your understanding of how money works, you need to know what to do with it. The next level is having that energy and enthusiasm, the *vigor*, to reach your financial goals. And with vigor comes vision. That outward vigor might look like joining and checking in with an accountability group and setting up your accounts a certain way. It might mean taking a financial literacy course. It definitely means reading this book!

One thing about financial literacy is that it does put you in a place where you now become calm and confident. One thing that I have noticed about leading such a large group of women in this financial literacy movement is that they become better equipped to shift from fear to fearlessness. This has been a rewarding outcome of being in this space with so many women. To watch women move from the conditioned state of self-sacrificing, where we put everybody before ourselves, to protecting their investments and having fun watching them grow is an added benefit. We all know the phrase "put on your own oxygen mask first," and it's just as true with finances as it is with an aircraft emergency. You have to secure your financial life before using your resources to help others. To put it another way, you can't help fill up someone else's cup if yours is empty.

Two of the biggest pitfalls about women and investing is that 1) they often don't feel like they can afford to, and 2) they don't want to take the risk because—you guessed it!—they can't afford to lose money. However, the fear of losing keeps you from winning. True, you may not trust or feel like you know where to start. Luckily, this book will help put you in a position to learn where to invest.

Many women tell me that investing seems as risky as gambling, but there is a difference between gambling and calculated risk. Gambling implies luck without skill or strategy. Investing is a risk, but with skill and strategy you can minimize your exposure and reap maximum benefits. With women being highly risk-averse, we don't want to touch anything.

The more risks you take, the luckier you become.

You have to be comfortable with taking more risks with your money. Fidelity Investments found that 65 percent of the women in their survey who were offered investment guidance in their workplace did not seek it out.[8]

We live in an information-rich society. From television to the internet's multiple platforms, women are being overwhelmed when it comes to making investment decisions. How do you figure out what information will actually help you when you are bombarded with, "Do this. Do that. Put your money here. Put your money there"?

Who do you trust? Who do you go to? Where do you start? My job is to help you cut through the noise and give you just what you need to make your money grow for your near-term and long-term goals.

Okay, I have made my case. I think you are ready to dive in.

Do you have a new mindset? Check.

Affirmations? Check.

Let's get started building the financial life that you desire.

FEARLESS FIGURES
Saundra D. Davis, MSFP, APFC, FBS

Saundra is a spiritual, financial auntie that you can turn to when your mind wants to shift into scary. As a US Navy veteran, financial coach, educator, and consultant, she smoothly aids to center your breathing and calm your beliefs around the bad stories we tell ourselves about having the money we deserve.

"Learn the lesson, leave the shame."

As a teen mother, Saundra had to learn many lessons around struggle and strife, but seeks to help others move past the shame and guilt of financial mistakes in order to receive financial abundance. She has been on a mission to change the mindset of Black women when it comes to money.

Don't let the calming voice of Saundra fool you. Not one to sugarcoat anything, she's a mighty force to be reckoned with, ensuring that women walk confidently and with clarity toward their financial desires. Always looking for the positive, she directs the ladies of the Queens of Capital Investment Mastermind to focus on energy that serves to bring joy and remove mental barriers that get in the way of the financial commitments we make with ourselves.

Making others face their financial fears and forgive themselves for financial mistakes is the skill that Saundra so eloquently weaves

into her sessions. Her formula for financial freedom: discipline ac-
companied by structure. Saundra says, "Having consistency is most
often what gets us to freedom."

Want to get on the other side of financial struggle? Saundra helps
women home in on their vision, be kind to themselves during the
process, and celebrate the small wins along their way to financial
independence. No wonder she's been called the financial coach's
coach.

MONEY MOVES

Complete the activity at the end of this chapter, "Five Financial
Success Affirmations." Retrain your brain to believe that you
can make the money you desire.

SUCCESS SQUAD

Personal Board of Advisors

These are your close friends and mentors who will tell it to you
straight, even when you're slacking off. They genuinely want to
see you win. My personal board of advisors includes my financial auntie, Gail Perry-Mason, First Vice President of Investments at Oppenheimer Investments and coauthor of *Girl, Get
Your Money Straight.*

Money Mentor

There's most likely someone in your circle of influence who has
a financial life that you admire and want to learn from. Lean in
to this person and start off by asking small, non-intrusive questions, such as, "I'm looking to invest a portion of my bonus
money. How did you get started with investing?" You'd be

surprised at how much someone will open up to you and drop a couple of jewels to get you going in the right direction.

Motivational Coach

This is a financial cheerleader, who will cheer you on and let you know how proud they are of you on every step of your glow-up. This is a hype man (or woman) who can help to boost your confidence and have you pressing onward and upward in this money game.

ACTIVITY:
FIVE FINANCIAL SUCCESS AFFIRMATIONS

Let's put into practice what I have discussed so far. As I mentioned, affirmations are strong and firm words that we use with ourselves. Because words have strength and power, it is important that we use the ones that make us feel good and support either how we feel or want to feel. I shared with you three affirmations that I use regularly, and now I will give you a formula you can use to create your own. The list of possibilities is endless, but for now, let's begin with five of your own. Keep in mind, while not all affirmations include the word *money* or *finances*, they absolutely can and should! At the end of the day, you want to feel good, optimistic, and joyful about your life. When you do, your money will feel that, too!

Affirmation #1

My life is _____ filled with _____ and _____.

Affirmation #2

There is enough _____, _____, _____ and _____ for everyone.

Affirmation #3

Money flows into my life. Because I respect it, it respects me. With money, I _____.

Affirmations #4 and #5

Write your own affirmations in the lines provided. Remember to use words that are strong, affirming, and focus on the present. For example, you should avoid saying, "I used to feel sad, but now I am grateful." And instead say, "I am grateful for my present life." In that statement we can infer that maybe you had struggles in the past, but since you are in the present, that's where your energy is focused.

Affirmation #4

_____

_____

_____

Affirmation #5

_____

_____

_____

TWO

Little Bank, Big Bank

You can't deposit excuses.

I was eighteen when I opened my first checking account. After graduating high school, my best friend got her first real job as a personal banker at a regional bank. I remember her telling me, "Hey, you should open up a bank account." I didn't think that I would have much use for one. I didn't even know how they worked. I came from a family who "banked" with cash. My mother never had a checking account. She paid her bills with money orders at the local check cashing spot. But my best friend was smart, and I trusted her.

I had no idea what I was doing. I walked into the bank, said, "Hey, girl," and sat down and opened up my first checking and savings account. She even helped me order the cute little Bugs Bunny checks so that I could pay my bills and organize my finances electronically instead of using cash all of the time. As I said, I did not know how banks worked and I definitely had to learn the hard way. What I didn't know then was that she was changing my financial trajectory and my relationship to banks.

In this chapter, I'm going to talk a little bit about how you can really use savings as a foundation for good personal finance. *Cash is queen*—it's important that you have a safety net to help you with a foundation to becoming financially free. In order for you to be fearless with banking, you have to know how to play the game. Sis, your bank account should match your handbag. Don't go out buying expensive handbags or expensive anything until you get your money up in your bank accounts.

> Your bank account should
> at least match your handbag.

Most of the time we look at banks as being a threat to our personal finance journey, but they actually play a pretty important role. We look at them as a threat to our financial prosperity because it's easy to make them out to be the big bad corporation. One thing about banks is that you want to ensure that you find a bank that does not "fee you" to death. A monthly fee here and a transfer fee there adds up. Let's not even start on overdraft fees. Even worse. The best thing to do when it comes to banking is to find banks that don't charge you for every little move your money makes. Remember, banks are just like you: they are trying to make money. But unlike you, they are a business and you are their business. Banks don't make a lot of money from payroll deposits or other day-to-day consumer transactions, so in order for them to make money, they must be able to pay you a lower interest rate on your savings and collect high fees. Make sure that your money won't be eaten every month by fees that are avoidable. Depending on the type of accounts you have, you may be able to negotiate those fees or have them waived. Bottom line, ask. You don't want to have to meet any minimum deposits to avoid paying fees. It's really that simple. After all, they can charge hefty fees, physical location hours can be inconvenient, and they have the nerve to offer unattractive interest rates on savings products. Why would anyone in their right mind want to park their money in a bank? It's the security for most because no one is getting rich from the anemic interest rates or taking world-class trips on their earnings from bank deposits.

Given the drawbacks from banking, I know that a large segment of the population shies away from using mainstream financial institutions. There's a fear of using banks and knowing how to maximize your relationship with a financial institution. Many simply choose not to even bother. According to the *2017 FDIC National Survey of Unbanked and Underbanked Households*, an estimated 16.9 percent of Black households were unbanked and an estimated 30.4 percent were underbanked.[1] Among unmarried female-led family households, 15.4 percent were unbanked, and 27.5 percent were underbanked.[2]

Unbanked refers to individuals who do not use a bank to keep money or make financial transactions. These individuals, according to the FDIC study, are more likely to be Black or Hispanic with lower levels of education. When individuals don't use a bank for transactions, they are more likely to pay high fees for services that would either be low-cost or free. An example would be paying a utility bill. In a banked scenario, an individual could use their bank's bill pay feature and pay the bill with the touch of a button. An unbanked individual might go to a check-cashing store and have the bill paid there for a fee.

Underbanked is a term that describes individuals who have a bank account, but primarily use outside establishments, like check-cashing stores, to make financial transactions. This also includes paying bills in cash. As you can see, if you are a person of color without formal education, or an unmarried woman in that same demographic, you might be at risk for either being unbanked or underbanked. Coming out of high school, I was unbanked because that's what I saw around me. My mother, also unbanked, was one of the women heading up her own household. Had she had a checking account and support on how to use one to her advantage, she could have used a bank's services to help her instead of being afraid that they would take what little money she had.

Despite the perception of banks, they are necessary and can be used in our favor. As the world becomes more connected online, there are ways for us to access our money without some of the inconveniences of the past. Changes in technology over the last two decades have improved how we access our money, move our money, and multiply our money. Despite the tech revolution sweeping across banks, you still want to find a bank where you feel comfortable enough to want to develop a relationship with key employees. They should want your business despite enhanced technology, new entrants, and stiff competition. Banks are well aware that you have more choices of where you can park your money. There are many banks that cater to the ethical, cultural, and professional considerations of our diverse population. There are Black-owned banks, banks that serve immigrant populations (especially from Asia), virtual banks (banks without a brick-and-mortar store), and credit unions that serve specific professions like teachers, firefighters, and members of the military.

Once you have decided on the type of bank to work with, it's time to get your money organized. Getting your money organized helps to save time and costly mistakes. You can also monitor and track your savings to check if you are meeting your savings target or if you need to make modifications along the way. Let's review a few basic areas of banking.

1. Types of banks and financial institutions
2. Savings account types
3. Savings products

You can have up to $250,000 per account per person covered by the Federal Deposit Insurance Corporation, or FDIC insurance. If you are a married couple, it's up to $500,000 at an institution; however, you should not have that much money parked in a savings account unless it is on a temporary basis with plans to move those funds to make an investment or find a savings vehicle that will earn a higher rate of return on your money.

BANKS AND FINANCIAL INSTITUTIONS

There are a variety of banking institutions to safely hold your fortune. The more money you have at a financial institution, the better the treatment. Banks are really designed as nothing more than a pit stop until you have bigger dreams for your money. Let's briefly review the different types of banks that are available for you to save your money.

Retail Bank

Retail banks are designed for the everyday consumer. These are banks with physical locations. They can have worldwide, national, regional, or local locations. The upside to big banks is that they have large networks, providing accessibility to ATMs and branches, with 24/7 customer service as well as user-friendly mobile apps for you to take care of your banking needs while on the go. Citibank, Chase, and Capital One are among the largest retail banks.

The downside with retail banks is that they do not have savings products that are going to pay you a reasonable rate of interest. The rates on the savings offerings at big banks tend to be low.

Banks are where you park your money
until you have bigger dreams for it.

Want to know if your money is safe and insured at the bank? Use the FDIC's Electronic Deposit Insurance Estimator (EDIE) at https://edie.fdic.gov.

Online Bank

These banks typically have no physical locations, but may have ATMs available for deposits and withdrawals. Online banks pass higher interest rates on to you, making their savings products slightly more attractive than retail banks since they have reduced overhead and operational expenses. But it'll cost you one to two days to transfer your money back to your retail bank, if funds are needed. Ally Bank and Discover are a couple of online banks to consider.

These days with online banking as our new normal, you want to be able to have a bank where you can do your transactions from the convenience of your phone, including mobile check deposits, wire transfers, and various other transactions.

An online bank will have checking, savings, credit cards, and loans comparable to a retail bank or credit union. However, the savings annual percentage yield (APY) is a little higher and may be more attractive than your local retail bank.

Want to find an online savings account that is going to provide you with the highest savings rate possible? You can always check out http://bankrate.com.

Credit Union

Similar to a retail bank, credit unions are not-for-profit organizations that are owned by their members and are exempt from paying federal taxes. Generally, the members have something in common such as attending the same university, working in the same profession, or living in the same community. Credit unions offer many of the same services as retail and online banks, but may have limited accessibility when it comes to locations. You can deposit up to $250,000, which is protected by the

National Credit Union Administration (NCUA). You can use credit unions just as you would a regular retail bank. Credit unions have locations in your area as opposed to across the country.

Brokerage Firm

Brokerage accounts are available at investment banks and they are good places to keep your savings. In brokerage accounts, you can handle everyday banking transactions such as paying bills and making mobile check deposits. The added benefit to brokerage accounts is that you can also invest in stocks, bonds, and funds. Many investment banks offer a cash management account to help you park your savings, making it easier to have all your funds at one place for savings and investing. If you have balances of $100,000 to $250,000 or more, it is worth looking into having your funds in a brokerage account to take advantage of additional services, such as private client banking. Morgan Stanley, Merrill Lynch, and Fidelity are a few of the most common investment banks that offer brokerage accounts. Below, you will find a short list of brokers and what makes them uniquely different when choosing a broker.

BROKERAGE FIRM	BEST KNOWN FOR	WEBSITE
Fidelity	Best overall and best for beginners	https://fidelity.com
TD Ameritrade	Best trading platform and best customer service	https://tdameritrade.com
E*Trade	Best mobile trading	https://etrade.com
Charles Schwab	Best IRA accounts and best broker podcast	https://schwab.com
Ally Invest	Best easy-to-use website	https://ally.com/invest
Merrill Edge	Best rewards from bank broker	https://merrilledge.com
JPMorgan	Best bank and investing all-in-one platform	https://www.chase.com/personal /investments/online-investing

Source: Stockbrokers.com

SAVINGS ACCOUNT TYPES

You should have three types of savings accounts: emergency fund, short-term, and medium-term. Retirement savings are long-term and we'll discuss that in chapter 6. Let's walk through how to set up your savings.

SAVINGS ACCOUNT TYPE	DURATION	SAVINGS PRODUCT	INSTITUTIONS
Emergency fund	1 month	Traditional savings account	Retail Bank Credit Union
	2–24 months	High-yield savings	Online bank Brokerage
Short-term savings	Up to 12 months	Traditional savings account	Retail bank Credit union Brokerage
Medium-term savings	1–3 years	Online high-yield savings Money market accounts CDs	Online bank Brokerage

Emergency Funds (Up to 24 Months)

I get a lot of questions from clients about how much they should actually save in an emergency fund. A good rule of thumb is anywhere from three to twenty-four months. The amount of your safety net is dependent upon how much time it would take you to bounce back from the loss of a job or other interruption, such as a break in your employment or to care for a family member. You can ask yourself this question: "If my income were to suddenly stop, how long would it take me to bounce back?"

Short-Term Savings (Up to 12 Months)

Savings for an important expense such as car registration, paying taxes, buying a new car, or taking a vacation in a year should be categorized as short-term savings. These funds should be kept liquid and should not be invested in the stock market.

Medium-Term Savings (1 to 3 Years)

Savings for a remodeling project, a wedding, or a down payment on a new home can be categorized as medium-term savings. Planning on giving your employer a pink slip? Want to start your own business or travel for a few months? You will need to financially prepare to do this. Medium-term savings should be earmarked for these types of goals.

SAVINGS PRODUCTS

Overall, savings products leave much to be desired when it comes to interest rates and annual percentage yields (APYs), but provide peace of mind when it comes to liquidity and accessibility of your money. Liquidity means that your money is fluid; it is not tied up with other investments or subject to withdrawal fees and taxes. Accessibility means your money is readily available and within reach.

Let's take a brief look at a few commonly used savings products.

Traditional Savings Accounts

A savings account is a basic type of account where you can deposit and make withdrawals with relative ease. It's one step up from tucking thousands of dollars under your mattress or carrying around wads of cash in your Louis Vuitton bag. You can earn a pittance of interest, definitely not enough to write home about. But the good news is that your money is federally insured up to $250,000 per account owner by the FDIC.

High-Yield Savings Accounts

For your emergency funds and medium-term savings, look to high-yield savings accounts offered by online banks. With the national average interest rate for savings accounts hovering around 0.06 percent as of this writing, high-yield savings accounts want to attract your money by offering up to seven times greater APYs than the national average on basic savings accounts. With higher yields, your money can make money faster—pushing you to your savings goals with a little more speed.

Money Market Accounts (MMAs)

A money market account is a blend of a savings account and a checking account. It looks like a savings account because you're able to get a slightly higher APY on your balance than a regular savings account. On the other hand, it functions like a checking account, allowing you to make up to six withdrawals in a statement period. MMAs are offered at retail banks, online banks, and credit unions. You may have to meet minimum deposit amount requirements such as $1,000 or $10,000 to take advantage of the higher APY, but there are money market accounts available with $0 deposit requirement. Either way, your money is FDIC-insured up to the limits, per account holder.

Certificate of Deposit

A certificate of deposit (CD) is a type of savings account offered by banks and credit unions. In exchange for locking your money up for a predetermined length of time (from 3, 6, or 12 months up to 10+ years), the bank will offer you a higher, guaranteed interest rate than on your basic savings account. When you open a CD, you choose how long you want to commit your funds. The longer the term you select, the higher the interest amount paid at maturity. Make sure you're able to stick to the term, because if you need to access the money in a CD, you may have to pay a penalty that could wipe out any interest you would have had coming to you and possibly some of your principal. You can expect to pay a higher fee depending on how far away you are from the maturity date. Once you hit the maturity date, the bank gives you a small window of time (called a grace period)

of about five to seven days to withdraw your money or find another savings product. If you miss the window, the bank will
take that as you're wanting to renew your CD for the same
length of time at whatever the going rate happens to be. If
you're not sure about tying your money up for a long period of
time, then look for no-penalty CDs or build a CD Ladder.

Build a CD Ladder

Excess cash over and above what you may need for emergency
purposes can be saved using a CD Ladder strategy. With a CD
Ladder, you get liquidity coupled with a slightly higher rate of
return on cash, which would otherwise earn very little in a regular savings account. Essentially, you buy multiple CDs with
varying maturity dates, where your money gets to take advantage of current rates as each CD reaches maturity. When building a CD Ladder, you want to decide the longest amount of time
you're willing to commit and then work your way down to
shorter maturity dates.

For example, let's say you had $10,000, were willing to go out
four years on your longest CD, and each CD would mature in
one-year increments (see figure 1). Here's how you could build
your CD Ladder:

- $2,500 in a one-year CD
- $2,500 in a two-year CD
- $2,500 in a three-year CD
- $2,500 in a four-year CD

Each year that a CD matures, you can renew it for the longest
term (in this example it would be for another four-year term),
and start the ladder all over again. Wash, rinse, and repeat. You
can set up ladders for as little as one year and for as long as ten
years, or whatever the longest duration is available at the financial institution. Find out how your money will grow with a CD

Ladder using the Ally Bank Quick CD Ladder Calculator: https://www.ally.com/bank/cd-ladder/quick-calculator.html.

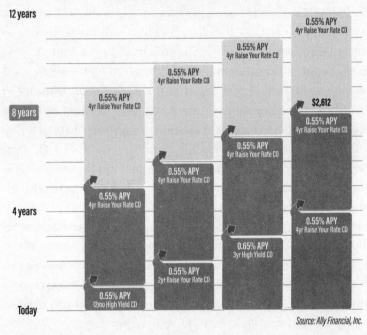

Figure 1

Want to build a custom CD Ladder? Check out Fidelity's CD Ladder Builder at https://fixedincome.fidelity.com/ftgw/fi /FILanding#tbcds|treasury|cd-new-issue|all.

OTHER TYPES OF SAVINGS PRODUCTS

Now that we've covered the most common savings products, let's take a peek at some nontraditional savings vehicles that may provide you with more attractive APYs. Many savers overlook these products because you may have to purchase them through a broker or third party, with the exception of a Roth IRA.

Roth IRA

Heads will turn and eyes will roll on this one, but you can use a Roth IRA for savings *and* investing for retirement. Contributions made to a Roth IRA have been taxed, allowing you to withdraw money that you've deposited into the account. As long as you avoid withdrawing any earnings before turning 59½ years of age or any earnings that haven't been in the account for at least five years (whichever comes last), your money is free to move when you're ready. More on this subject in chapter 6.

Fixed Annuity

A fixed annuity is similar to a CD, but this savings product is offered through an insurance company instead of a bank or credit union. You get to select the term, and fixed annuities typically pay a higher guaranteed rate than CDs. The interest grows tax-deferred, allowing your money to compound faster. However, the terms typically start at five-plus years and the penalties (called a surrender charge) are pretty stiff if you need to withdraw your money before the expiration date. Unlike CDs, you're able to withdraw up to 10 percent of the balance each contract year penalty-free. Fixed annuities are not FDIC-insured, so if you're considering this savings vehicle, ask the insurance broker about the company's rating to ensure you're saving with a reputable firm.

Cash Value Life Insurance

Funds accumulated in a cash value life insurance policy can be used for emergency purposes. As a policyholder, you can borrow cash against the policy, tax-free, while reducing the amount of the death benefit, in most cases. Although there is a nominal interest payment applied, cash value life insurance policies can be looked at as a source of emergency funding, if you need to get access to cash in a hurry.

HOW MUCH MONEY
SHOULD YOU KEEP IN THE BANK?

Your checking account should be set up for you to use for everyday transactions, such as paying bills, buying groceries, eating out, entertainment, and things like that. You should have at least one month of savings in a savings account at a retail bank or credit union. Anything more than one month of savings should be parked in an online high-yield savings account. For example, if you have three months of savings, one month should be in a savings account in a retail bank or credit union and the other two months should be parked in an online high-yield savings account.

HOW MUCH SHOULD YOU HAVE SAVED?

You should aim to beat the national average and save at least 20 percent of your after-tax income and raise that at least 1 to 2 percent a year. You want your savings to set you up to go from surviving to thriving. With that, let's look at how much you should save by age.

In Your Twenties

If you are in your twenties, you should aim to get in the habit of saving. Ideally, you should save a minimum of 10 percent a year and increase it 2 percent every year to account for inflation until you have built up a sizable safety net. In your twenties, you're just coming out of college. You're trying to settle on a career. You may have changed jobs, moved, gone back to school for more education, and so on. However, in spite of these natural fluctuations in your life, you should still get in the habit of learning how to save a minimum of 10 percent a year, no matter how often you switch jobs.

In Your Thirties

When you get to your thirties, life is underway. You have most likely figured out a career. You may have gotten married, had children, or both. Now you need to have at least one year's worth of living expenses covered. If you do not have at least one year's worth of living expenses covered, then you need to accelerate your savings to get there.

In Your Forties

You may have children that are small, school-age, or older and getting ready to leave the nest. You have probably gotten to a point in your career where you have maximized the amount of money you're going to make on your job.

At this point, you should aim to have three to ten times your living expenses. If you are not there, you should be saving to a point where it is painful. If you are not at the level of savings that will cover three to ten times your living expenses, then you need to find ways in which to accelerate your savings to meet this goal. If the goal is to be fearless with your finances, you have to get over the fear of saving money to meet your financial objectives.

In Your Fifties

Most likely you have gotten to a point where you are an empty nester. The children have left. You have reached an optimal point in your career. You may have started a business. You may have made some expensive purchases. You may have bought a Tesla with all the bells and whistles. You may have taken a trip around the world and now you are really focused on saving for retirement. You've got to "turn up" your retirement savings. This will allow you to get to financial freedom faster. In your fifties, you should aim to have seven to thirteen times your annual expenses. Again, if you have not reached that, make sure you accelerate your savings in order to do so.

In Your Sixties

Now you can see that retirement is on the horizon. In your sixties, you are excited about not having to work and you have probably reduced your living expenses. Now, you should definitely be at a point where you have accumulated close to twenty times your annual living expenses in order for you to actually no longer have to work. If you can get to that before your sixties, you are doing an excellent job at savings and you need this amount because at some point you'll start to draw down your savings. Therefore, if you never make any interest on your savings account, you need to be able to have enough money to withdraw every year for the rest of your life.

SAFETY NET SECRETS

Building a safety net of cash is equivalent to building a foundation on a house. You'll need this to move from survival to stability to surplus. Having a healthy stash of cash is really important to set the stage for financial independence. The following are some tips that I want to provide to help you accelerate and maximize your savings outside of what you would normally save after you receive your paycheck. There are ways in which you can do that.

Safety Net Secret #1

The first tip is to have a credit card that provides cash-back rewards. If you have a credit card that you use for everyday spending, you most likely will get cash back for certain types of purchases such as gas, groceries, and restaurants. You want to use that cash back to fund your emergency fund or short-term savings. You may want to look at checking accounts that provide you the ability to "keep the change." If you use your debit card, it rounds up your purchases. I suggest you move that money into a savings account, automatically. That way, you put your savings on autopilot to help you make up the gap, to get to your savings goal faster.

Safety Net Secret #2

Another safety net secret to funding your savings is to set up direct deposits to go directly to your online, high-yield savings account. Often, we have all the money come directly into our checking account from our paychecks, but if you have the ability to have your payroll deposits split up, you should have a percentage of that go directly into a savings account for you.

Safety Net Secret #3

If your bank isn't working for you, don't be afraid to switch to a credit union or a bank with fewer penalties and fees! Some of you reading this right now might be uncomfortable with the idea of switching banks out of the fear (there's that word again) that we are going to make the wrong choice. It's a hassle to change our automatic deposits or debits and we are creatures of habit. If our bank isn't terrible, then we stay because it's easier than making the switch.

Safety Net Secret #4

If you are a married couple with two incomes, you can use one income to pay all of the household expenses and then use the second income to save aggressively. You can get to your savings target expeditiously—within five to six years—if you work together to save, aggressively.

Safety Net Secret #5

Another strategy is, if you are a single parent, you may have to find other ways outside of your W-2 income to boost your savings. Because, honestly speaking, it's very difficult to save aggressively when you have children. But having children can definitely motivate you to find additional sources of income to meet your aggressive savings goal. As a teacher, I taught summer school, covered classes during my free period, tutored, was a cheerleading coach, and collected a stipend as an after-school math and science advisor. I didn't do these all at the same time, but over the course of the school year, I used my time on-site to bring in some side hustle income that fit my mommy schedule. Lastly, you should earmark a portion of any child support and/or child tax credits you receive and allocate that to savings, as well.

FEARLESS FIGURES
Sheena Allen, Founder of CapWay Bank

Sheena packs a big punch, as a young Black woman in tech. She's blazing trails to give access and create a way for citizens who have been financially underserved, overlooked, or misunderstood to have a positive relationship with banking. As the founder of her second startup, CapWay Bank, this *Forbes* 30 under 30 and *Inc.*'s Female Founders 100 recipient is on the move to create an inclusive financial system that solves the problems created and continued by traditional banking institutions.

Her first tech startup, Sheena Allen Apps, had in excess of six million app downloads. How did she do it? She hired developers to bring her vision to life, even turning down a paltry five-figure offer to buy one of her apps, all while obtaining a double major in psychology and film at the University of Southern Mississippi.

> "Don't focus on trying to prove everybody else wrong.
> Focus on proving yourself right."

This southern belle and generational wealth builder had a TEDx appearance where she shed light on alternative, yet predatory, banking options such as check cashing, payday lenders, and pawnshops that continually set up shops in low-income neighborhoods, further stifling economic growth in targeted communities.

With more than thirty million Americans "underbanked," and more than 70 percent of Americans who are living paycheck to paycheck and struggling with a possible overdraft fee, Sheena's launch of a digital bank is no small feat, but she is fearless and up to the assignment. A mobile-first platform, CapWay provides debit cards to an audience not familiar with (or untrusting of) the traditional banking system. The debit cards are combined with financial education, saving tools (called Money Goals), and opportunities to help guide users on a path to financial health. Backed by Backstage Capital, founded by Arlan Hamilton, Sheena looks to bring brighter financial days to those who unfortunately know what it's like to bank while Black.

MONEY MOVES

Establish and organize your accounts to be successful at managing your money. Organization of your money matters will build confidence and provide clarity in knowing where all your money is parked or moving.

SUCCESS SQUAD

Banks have a variety of key employees who are available to serve your banking needs.

Personal Banker

Get to know a personal banker to find out about current interest rates on savings products and any new features recently rolled out at the bank. The personal banker is the gatekeeper to many of the key employees you'll eventually want to meet and greet.

Mortgage Specialist

Ask the personal banker to introduce you to the mortgage representative, even if you're not in the market to purchase a home. Asking questions about current interest rates and home purchasing programs starts to build a relationship with this key employee.

Small Business Representatives

If you own your own business or you're considering taking the leap into entrepreneurship, you'll want to meet the representative for merchant services and get contact information for the bank's small business lending representative.

Private Wealth Advisor

If the bank or credit union offers investment services, be sure to get acquainted with the bank's designated financial advisor. This specialist can make you aware of new investment-related services and may be able to eliminate fees or offer reduced fees based on the amount of financial assets you hold at the bank. The point is that you want to start to build relationships and make it easier to put a face to a name.

THREE

Credit Card Come Up

Give yourself a little bit of credit.

You just can't dismiss the value of using other people's money to build wealth. Although there are several credit bureau gurus on the scene, they seem to only tell you how to build and boost your credit score. It's important to put credit cards to work for you on your wealth-building journey. The game has changed.

Building wealth takes time, but if you get the right cards to suit your spending patterns and behaviors, you can live a wealthy lifestyle at a fraction of the cost. Credit card rewards come in one of three ways: airline miles, hotel points, or cash back. Cash-back points, miles, and statement credits are really just other forms of currency. Lean in and take note of a few things as you use your credit cards to build wealth.

DEBIT CARD VS. CREDIT CARD

Debit and credit cards are like salt and sugar, respectively: on the surface, they look alike, but they work (and taste!) very differently.

Here's a rundown of why credit cards can be sweeter than swiping your debit card.

- Credit building
- Protection on purchases, such as warranties
- Getting rewards and points
- Thirty-day interest-free loan
- Secure hotel and rental car reservations

Swipe your debit card and use your hard-earned cash for virtually nothing in exchange outside of convenience, if you insist. At the end of the day, using your credit cards, fearlessly, far outweighs the benefits of using reward and premium debit cards.

> Points, miles, and credits are other
> forms of currency. Run it up!

TYPES OF CREDIT CARDS

Let's take a look at each type of credit card that you should have in your wallet. Again, being fearless about money means using your cards in a way that makes sense for you. Move about living your daily life, but with some perks thrown in there, too.

Cash-Back Cards

Want to live a fearless financial lifestyle without paying tons of cash out of pocket? Cash-back cards give you the opportunity to earn money back on your purchases. Sometimes, they will match or provide you with anywhere from 1 percent to 6 percent or more. You should definitely have a cash-back rewards card that will allow you to receive either cash back in your account or a statement credit toward reducing your overall balance.

Look for a card that pays no less than 2 percent on purchases. Many cash-back cards will have a cap either monthly, quarterly, or annually, where they will allow you to receive cash back up to a certain amount over a predetermined period. Bottom line, be sure that you understand how your cash back can be received. Please note, if you receive more than $600 in cash back in the form of a check, it will count as additional income for IRS tax purposes and you may receive a 1099 miscellaneous form from your credit card provider. If you do that, your income will be reportable. However, if the cash is applied to your statement balance or if it is deposited into an account, then the IRS views that as a rebate, which is not taxable. Cash-back cards are great if you use them for everyday purchases. But, once you hit your cash-back cap, you may want to switch up your rewards strategy and use a different card.

You can always elect to have those funds deposited in an account where you can invest and buy stock ETFs and index funds. This is a great way for you to make money on things that you would spend on everyday living expenses, anyway.

Consider a cash-back card like the Fidelity Visa Rewards card that pays you 2 percent cash back. The cash back is automatically deposited into a Fidelity account that you must open prior to having the card. You may ask Fidelity to run you your money in a check, but let's change the narrative and see that Fidelity can help you find the money to invest where you otherwise wouldn't on your own volition.

Airline Miles Cards

Another type of rewards credit card is one that racks up airline miles. You want to be able to redeem miles that you have accumulated to reduce, if not eliminate, money spent out of your pocket for traveling. Now, who wouldn't want free travel? There is a catch: if it costs less for you in cash to pay for your flight outright, it's best to do that. However, if it is better for you to redeem a certain number of miles, as opposed to paying cash, then by all means, use your miles instead. The objective is to accumulate as many points as you possibly can to offset flight- and travel-related expenses.

Miles you earn from everyday purchases can be applied to roam the earth on free flights and other travel accommodations using your credit card. If you have a card that allows you to run up airline miles, it is best to go through the particular airline associated with the card. Is it best to go through that credit card's website to reserve those travel benefits? Yes. It is best to go through that credit card's website to redeem and purchase airline tickets and travel-related items, to get the best bang for your buck. Additionally, credit card companies will provide an additional bonus for booking travel through their portal. When you use their credit card website to make your travel arrange- ments, some credit card companies offer up to an additional 25 percent and upward of an additional 50 percent bonus in the miles. *Can you say vacay me?*

The other good thing about airline miles credit cards is that many of them are part of travel groups. This allows you to trans- fer your points from one airline to another airline in order to utilize those points.

When it comes to airline miles, one of the best cards for get- ting to the travel bag is the Chase Sapphire Reserve card, or even the Chase Sapphire card. With these cards, you can earn three points for every dollar you spend that can be applied to- ward travel or hotel points. Take a look at a card such as the American Express Platinum personal credit card, where you can earn five times the points on flights and prepaid hotels on amextravel.com, as well as one point on other purchases. The card does come with a hair-raising $695 annual fee, but the re- ward welcome bonus equates to one hundred thousand points. With all of the perks you get as a card-carrying member of the

Platinum Amex gang, the welcome bonus more than pays for itself in the first year of use.

Some cards also allow you to receive free flight upgrades. You can even kick it like a queen in airport lounges at some of the busiest airports around the world.

Hotel Points

Hotel points are great for those travel cards that allow you to accumulate points to earn free nights at dozens of hotels across the world.

Many of these hotels and hotel groups will allow you to stay at a number of different chains. You have the Marriott Hotels, Hilton Honors, and the World of Hyatt just to name a few. Your cards may be able to redeem your points for a stay on the Amalfi coast or in a tree house in Costa Rica. You can get additional benefits such as special offers for breakfast, excursions, upgrades to suites, and additional nights during your stay.

Once you have accumulated a substantial number of points, you might even have the benefit of transferring those points to partners that you can use for additional award flights and hotels. Again, the objective is to use these points, miles, and cashback incentives to reduce the amount of cash that is actually coming out of your own pocket.

If you have a large family and spend what it costs to feed a small village in Thailand buying groceries, make sure that you get a card that provides you with bonuses toward your groceries and other expenses that you would normally buy anyway. Expenses for gas can count toward receiving two, three, and even five times the number of points. That family trip to Disney World to see Mickey Mouse will hit different if you're able to stay at the Walt Disney World Resort and ride "It's a Small World" for nearly free.

SEVEN RULES FOR BUILDING
WEALTH WITH CREDIT

Chances are, if you are reading this book, you know how credit works, or at least you think you do. But it never hurts to remind investors like yourself that credit is key and interest rates are good when they benefit you, and bad when they cost you. For example, when you have a high-yield savings account, that's good because your investment is earning interest. It's not good when you have a credit card and for every dollar you spend, you are charged anywhere from 14 to 24 percent daily average. That's a lot of money over time, money you could use for saving or investing.

> Make using other people's money to build
> wealth seem natural and seamless.

Strong credit builds wealth over time because you are saving money by not constantly turning hard-earned money over to fees and penalties. Banks and other financial institutions want to know that, over time, they can trust you with their money. Are you using all of your available credit? Are you paying more than the minimum balance due? Are you paying your bills on time? These may seem like obvious or even trivial notions, but generational wealth requires time, patience, and discipline. It also requires careful reading of the fine print so you don't get caught flat-footed with fees or interest rates. You are also able to teach those around you (children, nieces or nephews, or even your own parents) to pay attention to the opportunities and the pitfalls of credit and investing.

I have a few rules to get you going.

Rule 1—Don't carry a balance.
Pay off your credit card every month. When you carry a balance, you incur interest and potential late fees. Carrying a balance, interest, and late fees negate the purpose of using credit cards that have rewards and incentives attached to them.

Rule 2—Don't pay late fees or interest.
Make sure you make your payments on time, preferably before the statement date. If you make your payments on time, it's going to allow you to use your credit card limits as a thirty-day interest-free loan. Take advantage of paying your credit cards on time and, if possible, make payments twice a month.

Rule 3—Don't have just one type of rewards credit card.
This is key to accumulating credit card points, miles, gas, and cash in this credit card rewards game. Diversify the types of cards that you have and be mindful of the plastic (or titanium) you keep in your wallet.

Rule 4—Don't let rewards and points expire.
Make sure you understand the benefits that come with each card that you open and make sure that you do not let miles or points expire. You spent hard-earned money to get them and you don't want to leave money on the table.

Cash-back points, miles, and statement credit is really just another form of currency. You don't want it to slip through your fingers like water.

Rule 5—Don't let welcome and sign-up bonuses slip away.
Those bonuses will fall by the wayside. When you are researching and looking into opening up a credit card that comes with a onetime bonus, it's really a catalyst to earning more miles, points, and rewards on a card. For example, let's say a card is offering you a onetime bonus of sixty thousand miles or

one hundred thousand points, if you spend a certain amount within a three-month period. Make sure that you have figured out what purchases you're going to make to receive the sign-up or the welcome bonus within that specified period of time. These bonuses can add up to hundreds of dollars, if not more. You do not want to lose that bonus benefit by not paying attention to the criteria you have to meet in order to collect your benefits.

Rule 6—Don't turn your back on credit cards that have an annual fee.

Cards that have an annual fee come with so many bells and whistles, along with the ability for you to more than compensate for that annual fee in the form of rewards, incentives, referral bonuses, double points, and even free hotel weekend stays. If the annual fee doesn't sit well in your spirit, then there are cards that offer no annual fee or waive the fee for the first year. With a card that waives the fee for the first year, you get an opportunity to take the card out for a test run with minimal risk to your bottom line. Make sure that you read through and identify all of the benefits and features as well as the rewards and incentives you will receive in exchange for being a cardholder. The rewards and incentives that you receive far outweigh what you'll pay in the annual fee. If you get to use the card for one year and now it's time to pay up an annual fee, you can always call the credit card issuer and negotiate getting the annual credit annual fee waived.

Rule 7—Don't pay foreign transaction fees.

With travel cards be sure that you do not use cards that have a foreign transaction fee when using your card out of the country. A transaction fee of 3 percent can put a damper on your world travels. When you are traveling outside of the country, be mindful of cards that waive this foreign transaction fee. Credit card companies that are generous this way make their cards very attractive to use when you are traveling outside of the United States.

THREE RESPONSIBLE WAYS
TO USE A CREDIT CARD

I can't stress enough about using credit cards *responsibly*. There are several advantages to credit cards—powered by card issuers that hope to lead you to misuse your cards and overspend. Now that you're grown and may have performed plastic surgery by cutting up some previous cards, it's time to put the past behind you and put some money, trips, and perks in your fearless future. Below, I've listed a few other ways in which you can maximize your credit cards to make money for you and increase your wealth.

Add Authorized Users

You can add authorized users, depending on how long you have had your card and your utilization rate on your card. You can make money by charging people in need of a temporary credit boost the ability to be added to your credit card as an authorized user. Although I didn't charge my daughter (aka my broke best friend), I've added her to my card as an authorized user to assist with raising her credit score to learn how to utilize credit cards, qualify for an apartment, and purchase property. You can help someone boost their credit score for a short period of time. When you want to add an authorized user, whether it be a friend or family member, you can add them to your account. You can set spending limits and rack up credit card rewards when they spend using the card. This is a great way to help a friend in need, if you have great credit and they are looking to leverage your credit profile to raise their credit score.

Purchase and Resell Items

The second way in which you can earn money from your credit card is to purchase items at a discount and then sell them at a higher price. Wouldn't it be great to buy items at a lower price and then make a profit by reselling them at a higher price? Having a credit card allows you to use your limits in such a way where you can make multiple purchases of items and then make a profit by reselling those items at a higher price. You want to be sure that you are purchasing items prime for resale, including items that may be in high demand, such as newly released video game consoles or furniture items purchased at yard sales and refurbished for resale at a higher price point.

Use Your Card Frequently and Pay It Off

You can use one or more of your cards frequently, as close to the maximum credit limit allowed as you want, but always pay in full *prior* to the statement date. By using your cards in this manner, the card issuer will view you as a responsible consumer and will be inclined to raise your credit limits over a short period of time. Consider building a significant credit line with a card issuer. Becoming a favorable cardholder in the card issuer's eyes (rather, their algorithms), the sky can be the limit when it comes to your available credit line. A credit card goal might include getting consistent increases for your line of credit to cover a vehicle or real estate purchase on your credit card. That's what you call fearless!

Credit cards can be used as a tool to build wealth. Ultimately, it is best to make a thorough assessment of your overall spending patterns to identify which cards are best for you. It is an important part of having fearless finances to use other people's money (if only for thirty days or less), as another form of currency and to finance business activity to move the needle on your money. Rarely are we taught at a young age how to best manage our credit and not run up huge amounts of credit card debt. But if you are a responsible credit-card-carrying member and you have the income to support your purchases, then you also have the opportunity to make money off of your cards. Make using other people's money to build wealth seem natural and seamless. Be smart, yet fearless, about utilizing credit cards for the benefits, rewards, and incentives that they provide to help use short-term, interest-free capital that can afford you a certain type of lifestyle at a fraction of what others would pay in cash.

FEARLESS FIGURES
Arnita Johnson-Hall

From Section 8 to a seven-figure business, Arnita is unapologetic about her success in the credit repair realm. A wife and mother of five, she pulled herself up and out of poverty by turning her poor credit score into a profitable business after working diligently to improve her own credit rating.

Although she was employed, as a single mother she often found herself running out of money before the end of the month. To make her income stretch, she turned to government assistance to fill the gap. "After almost losing my life to a domestic violence incident with an ex-boyfriend, I was moved to a roach-infested, high-crime, government-assisted housing. I was a mom and wanted a better life for my daughter. That's when I made a vow to myself to become financially independent."

An investment in herself and in credit education was her ticket out of poverty. She voluntarily cut herself off of the government's handout and gave herself a leg up by working to improve her credit score. Using the knowledge she gained to boost her own score, she pivoted as a credit consultant where she helps others become financially literate with credit. It took her five years to go from making $12 an hour to making just $12,000 a year in her business.

Not one to back down, she pressed the gas on her business and ramped up her social media marketing to gain more than 250,000 followers, catapulting her to her first seven-figure year by 2016. She traveled to conferences and fearlessly grew her network, offering to assist others with improving their creditworthiness to unlock the door to financial freedom.

As the founder of AMB Credit and Luxurious Credit, she helps others launch and scale their very own credit repair enterprises.

MONEY MOVES

I have listed some resources to learn more about credit cards.

- Magnify Money—https://www.magnifymoney.com /blog/building-credit/minimize-risk-check-if-youre -pre-qualified-for-a-credit-card220647375/
- American Express Points—https://global .americanexpress.com/rewards
- Chase Credit Card Points—https://www.chase.com /personal/credit-cards/ultimate-rewards
- The Points Guy—http://thepointsguy.com, a blog dedicated to getting the most out of credit card rewards

Please note, if you are declined approval for a card, you have an opportunity to find out the company's reason for the denial, at a minimum. According to the Fair Credit Reporting Act, you are required to receive a letter by mail that outlines why you were declined approval.[1] The letter, called an *adverse action letter*, will give you your credit score, including the one used to approve/deny credit and a specific reason for the decline (for example, "too much existing debt"). Rather than seeing the adverse action letter as a setback, use it as a starting point to whip your credit profile into great shape.

Your second course of action can be to contact the card issuer's reconsideration line. I keep my credit file locked, and if applying for a card, it can trigger a denial on the basis that the credit bureau doesn't have access to my credit file. Call the credit bureau (or unfreeze your credit file online). By speaking with a credit card representative, they can review your application and grant a manual approval over the phone.

SUCCESS SQUAD

Speak with a personal banker at your retail bank or brokerage firm. They can review the benefits of the credit cards and assist with the application process.

PART 2

Fearless Flow
Stability

You've caught your financial footing, but you want to be sure to never slip into a personal recession again. In this section, the goal is to confidently move your financial needs beyond basic and build upon a solid, financial foundation. Knowing that your income more than covers your needs and that you've saved for financial storms will set you up nicely to put your money to work for you.

FOUR

Invest Like a Queen

Past performance is not an indicator of future results.

Investing is a critical component of reaching a level of financial freedom and fearlessness when it comes to your finances. Essentially, what you want when you invest is for your money to work for you, enabling you to sleep well at night. So why do women shy away from investing?

Generally speaking, financial security is important to women, more so than men. According to a US Bank survey, 46 percent of women value financial security, compared to 36 percent of men.[1] If financial security is important to women, then why do so many leave it up to their male counterparts to handle the investing? Women can increase their odds of gaining financial security through investing, as it's been proven that women are better investors than men. According to Fidelity's 2021 Women and Investing Study, over the last ten years, women have performed better than men by 0.4 percent (40 basis points).[2]

And yet, the fear of loss is keeping women from winning in the stock market. Only 19 percent of women feel confident

selecting investments that align with their goals.[3] But many will
buy a lottery ticket and invest in the dream of winning. Sis,
dreams do come true for one in three hundred million lottery
players. It's much better if you take your chances in the stock
market and beat the extreme odds of becoming a woman living
destitute.[4] Women tend to shy away from investing because
they're fearful of losing money. Women may not want to invest
in the stock market because when they tried it before, they lost
money. I get it. Nobody likes to lose money, especially me. Because women value security and safety over freedom and power,
many women would much rather sit on cash than invest in the
stock market; nearly half of women (47 percent) in the Fidelity
study have savings of $20,000 or more.[5] When it comes to our
finances, investing in the stock market is a key component to
growing wealth. You cannot save your way to prosperity and you
cannot meet your financial goals just by saving money your entire life. You must invest until your investments give you the income you need for life without having to work for it. We tend to
view investing as if we're handing our purses over to strangers.
That in and of itself can be a scary proposition. So how do you
overcome your fear of investing in a stock market and become
fearless when it comes to investing?

Change the narrative.

If the stranger was going to hand you back your purse and a few
other bags filled with cash, would you throw your bag their way?
This is how women need to view investing in the stock market.

Unsure of where to start? If you do not have the education on
how stocks work, there may be an intimidation factor. If you
don't know something, there is a greater likelihood that you will
fall back on what you *do* know. Many women will simply opt out
because they don't know how investing works. But we can
change the narrative here, too.

The longer you're in the investing game, the greater your odds
of financial success. Long-term investing requires endurance

and discipline. Long-term investing is really like watching paint dry—boring, but it can look so good. We need time in the market for our money to grow and help us achieve a level of fearlessness and flexibility. As women we don't have the luxury of spending a significant amount of time researching companies in order to decide where we should actually invest our money. Our family and work obligations are prioritized, leaving investing on the back burner. But we can no longer afford to put everything and everyone before us.

> You must invest until you have income for life,
>
> without having to work for it.

Start to look at stocks as self-care. View the time spent looking over your statements and accounts as a form of self-care. The amount of research required to invest in the stock market can be daunting, which is why a lot of women will allocate their time toward other things that are more interesting than picking up a prospectus to read.

How do you balance the risk of financial security, loss of funds, not knowing where to start, and the lack of time with the reward of investing in the stock market? By finding investments that you love. You have to get to a point where you love your investments. Sounds crazy, right? But do we give up on things that we love? Absolutely not.

There is a level of commitment that we have toward things that we deeply love and care about. If we love and care about freedom, flexibility, the ability to spend more time with people that we love, and not having financial concerns, then we must also learn to love our investments that will give us that type of lifestyle.

To become a fearless investor, you have to pick individual stocks and diversified funds. Let's take a look at both of these.

Before we break down individual stats in index funds, here are a few things to consider that can help you overcome your fear of investing. The more you earn, the more you learn. You put money in the market to have money in the market. This will allow you to better understand how much risk you're willing to take on. Now, I get it. There's no fun losing money, but it comes with the territory. And what you have to realize is that you have to have wins that far exceed your losses. The longer you stay in the game, the more your wins will outperform your losses.

Because we have so many responsibilities and obligations, we tend to want to control the remaining factors, variables, and conditions in our lives. The outcomes of the stock market are no different. Just know that it is impossible for you to outsmart and outperform the stock market. So, it's best to just decide on what you're going to buy and stick with it over the long run. This is why it's important for you to love your investments, because, over time, your investments will love you back. Since you can't control how the markets are going to react, one thing you should definitely be in total control of is allocating your investments. That might look like splitting up your funds into different asset classes to create diversification. Diversification is not about having all your eggs in the same basket, but making sure your eggs are in different colors: real estate, cash, stocks, bonds, precious metals, and so on.

> Diversification is having a nest full
> of eggs in different colors.

But no matter what, please don't beat yourself up. If you've missed out on becoming a multimillionaire because you didn't get in on Apple, Amazon, Tesla, or one of the other high-performing stocks, it's okay. There is money to be made everywhere. And now that you know better, you can do better. You

have to be in it to win and have to be in different types of investments in order for you to diversify your investment portfolio.

The other thing besides lack of time that keeps women from
investing is seeing losses in our account. Someone might say to
you, "it's not a paper loss until you sell it," but that isn't a very
rational way to think about losses. However, you have to stick
with it until those losses recover. You have to make sure that you
don't panic and let fear seep in to make you emotional about
the loss and actually sell the investment. If you sell too early, you
do not allow your investment to recover and most likely become
profitable down the line, which is why it's so important for you
to stick to a long-term investment strategy. Once you've overcome the fear, how do you actually set up your stock market
portfolio for the long term?

It's time to change the narrative that you tell yourself about
money. It's really important to understand that you have to tell
yourself positive things about investing money because there
are a few things that are going to be stable. It's going to be
your investing behavior, despite uncertainty in the market,
that will fuel your overall growth with investing in the stock
market.

LET'S TALK ABOUT INTEREST

When it comes to our finances, we'll need to have a conversation
about interest. In a nutshell, interest is this amazingly big thing
that can grow your money from a relatively small amount—over
time. About $81.5 billion of Warren Buffett's $84.5 billion net
worth came after he qualified for Social Security on his
sixty-fifth birthday.[6] I'm sure if you had started investing at ten
years old instead of playing with dolls or hide-and-go-seek, then
you might be on your way to becoming a quadrillionaire. The
amount of interest that you earn over time can be a significant
driver to building wealth.

You want to set your money up in a way that can provide free-dom and flexibility to you. That is the true advantage. We're going to talk about a couple of ways in which interest can help you meet your fearless financial goals. Let's take a look at simple interest vs. compound interest.

Simple Interest

Would you rather drive from Los Angeles to New York or catch a direct flight? Simple interest is similar to taking a cross-country road trip. You'll get there, eventually. In today's fast-paced world, simple interest will have your money stumbling down a single lane highway. Sis, this may not be the way to go if you're on your way to wealth in this lifetime. Simple interest is calcu-lated by taking the rate and multiplying it by only the principal of a loan, debt, or an investment.

For example, if you had $1,000 and a simple interest rate of 3 percent, you'd earn $30 each year. Your interest earnings will remain the same as long as the principal amount of $1,000 stays the same—so you'd earn $30 in year one, $30 in year two, and so on. After twenty years you'd have $1000 + ($30 x 20), so $1,600 total. And $600 in interest earnings in twenty years is like taking a slow boat to China.

From a debt repayment perspective, simple interest can be good. When applied to loans, simple interest keeps the total payment down because it never gets added to the amount of accumulated, but unpaid, interest. This allows you to pay down the debt quickly without the interest owed creeping up faster than you can pay it off. However, when it comes to investments, simple interest is typically unfavorable, like that long car ride from coast to coast, because your balance doesn't grow nearly as fast. Simple interest is not really something you should look at if you prefer exponential growth on your money.

Compound Interest

The second type of interest is compound interest. A famous, yet anonymous quote states, "Compound interest is the eighth wonder of the world. [S]he who understands it, earns it. [S]he who doesn't . . . pays it." Remember that direct flight from Southern California to New York? Yeah, that's compounding. Once that plane gets off the ground, you're on your way. The compounding potential of your money can accelerate the growth of your account balances. Compound interest is calculated by taking the rate and multiplying it on the accumulated, but unpaid, interest.

For example, if you had $1,000 and an annual compound interest rate of 3 percent, at the end of the first year you'll have $1,030. For year two, you'll earn interest on $1,030. That equals $30.90 in interest that year instead of an even $30.00. In year three, you'll earn interest on $1,060.99, and so on. After twenty years you would have $1,806.11 total.

I don't know about you, but I can use the extra $206.11 with the additional time I was able to buy back on my money.

However, depending on the situation, it can be a blessing or a curse. When applied to your savings (such as your money market accounts, certificates of deposit, and investments), compound interest can be quite beneficial to your long-term wealth-building strategy. However, when applied to any loans or other debt, compound interest is a curse on your financial plan.

BECOME A BAG LADY

Contrary to what Erykah Badu may have told you, being a bag lady will actually help you here. What you want to do is create three separate bags for your stock market investments: passive, active, and experiential.

Bag 1—Passive Portfolio

The first category is going to be your passive portfolio. This is where you set up your index funds, a low-cost basket of stocks. Index funds can be in your 401(k) or employer-sponsored retirement account. It could be in your IRA retirement account. You want to build up this passive part of your investment portfolio with automatic contributions from your paycheck. Pick a certain amount to invest every month and stick to it no matter what. Although index funds eliminate the need to perform research on individual companies because index funds passively track an index, you want to ensure you monitor the performance of the fund against your long-term investment goals and make adjustments accordingly. Your passive bucket will be the money that you basically put on autopilot and let it ride. Because it has a longer timeline, it can assume a higher risk due to the fluctuations in the economy and your portfolio being able to recover from downturns in the stock market.

Bag 2—Active Portfolio

The second part of your portfolio should be actively managed. This is where you can take a look at different stocks that you want to buy and hold. These are some of the stocks that you've come to know and love that you would feel comfortable holding on to for at least ten years. These could be stocks of companies whose products or services you use, or whose businesses you patronize.

Bag 3—Experiential

This third part of your investment portfolio would be where you may want to take on a bit more risk. You might buy a trending stock or into an Initial Public Offering (IPO), something that's a little higher risk, but you don't intend to hold it for the long term. If you want to use the money for short-term needs, this will allow you to avoid liquidating the passive and active bags of your portfolio.

ACCOUNT SETUP

You're probably asking, "Okay, Cassandra, that's all good, but where do I get started and open my accounts?" The passive part of your investment portfolio should be your retirement accounts. That's going to be your 401(k) and Individual Retirement Accounts, such as a Traditional IRA, Roth IRA, or a SEP IRA (Simplified Employee Pension) if you're self-employed. Any funds that will be allocated for long-term purposes should definitely go into passive accounts. Accounts such as your brokerage account and short-term investment accounts are going to be active. Your third account is your experiential account and should be placed with a discount broker. You can have all of these accounts with the same firm to clearly see how each one is performing.

Another question that gets posed quite a bit to me is, "Cassandra, how much do I need to get started?" The rule of thumb is to take a hundred minus your age.

$$100 - Age = \% \ of \ Disposable \ Income \ to \ Invest$$

That is the percentage that should be invested in stocks. For example, let's say you're forty years old. 100 minus 40 is 60. Therefore, 60 percent of your disposable income investments should be invested in stocks. Of this 60 percent, you can break it down further into your three bags:

- 60 percent passive
- 30 percent active
- 10 percent in your fun money account

If you want to reduce the short-term risk, you can increase the passive amount and have:

- 70 percent passive
- 20 percent active
- 10 percent in your fun money account

If you want to reduce the long-term risk of your portfolio, you can increase the active amount and allocate:

- 50 percent passive
- 40 percent active
- 10 percent in your fun money account

PAST PERFORMANCE IS NOT AN INDICATOR OF FUTURE RESULTS

We hear this so often because investing is a soft science. Investing can be emotional for you, especially when starting out on your investing journey. This is why it is hard to use past performance to predict what will happen next in the investment world. Yes, one thing certain is that things do change over time, and because of those changes, your investment strategies should change, too. The way you allocate your money should be ready for change over time.

It's time to change the narrative that you tell yourself about money. When you tell yourself to be fearful of money, that you're not good at math, or that your husband will handle all of the finances, your mind believes those things when it comes to your money. It's really important to understand that you have to tell yourself positive things about investing money. Because there are a few things that are going to be stable, it's going to be your investing behavior, despite uncertainty in the market, that will fuel your overall growth with investing in the stock market.

TYPES OF INVESTORS

Let's take a look at four types of investors to see which style best suits you.

Value Investor

Value investors are those who look for stocks that are undervalued by the market. These are companies that are "on sale" and can be purchased at a bargain deal. Value investors look for companies that are established, but may be going through a crisis. All companies go through transition periods, and the companies in question may be experiencing a little bit of a hiccup at the time. Value stocks include companies that are in the midst of restructuring, but at some point they will come out ahead and you were lucky enough to get in when these companies were going through a transition. If this sounds like you, then you may in fact be a value investor.

Growth Investor

A growth investor is someone who is seeking companies that they think will deliver above-average returns. These are companies that they feel are going to be innovative and are positioned at the right place at the right time, depending on what's going on in the current economy. These are companies that are introducing new products and services to the market based on technology or what's needed at the time. Growth investors find that technology and emerging companies fit this category of growth stocks.

Momentum Investor

A momentum investor is one who sets up a system of buying stocks that have had high returns over the past three to twelve months. They sell stocks that have had poor returns over the same three-to-twelve-month period. These are companies in which they might experience a huge surge, a huge spike in returns because of a product or an event or something of that nature that has caused the stock to boom. These are investors that look for companies that are on the cutting edge of new technology or perhaps pharmaceutical development. They could also be on the cutting edge of some sort of service. They could be companies that are taking advantage of a current economic event, such as a global pandemic. These are companies that will do well because they are stay-at-home stocks. These could be stocks that experience a significant amount of growth because of some sort of natural disaster in a particular region, or area, or a country that has to rebuild. Stocks that are tied to companies that are part of those rebuilding efforts could be looked at as momentum companies.

Dollar Cost Averaging Investor

The fourth type of investor is a dollar cost averaging investor. This investor looks to invest a flat amount in a particular sector, market, industry, or company.

Dollar cost investors believe that by investing the same amount on a consistent regular basis, you will reduce the impact on your investment of a stock going up or down over time. Many times, you will hear investors say "averaging down" when a stock's price falls. You will also hear terms like "averaging up." This is where you continue to buy even though the stock price continues to climb.

Dollar cost averaging seeks to take the emotion out of investing. It makes it so that you are investing no matter what the price happens to be. You are wedded to that company, or you are wedded to investing. Period.

The four most dangerous words in investing, as stated by investor John Templeton, are: "It's different this time." The state of the economy shifts and changes over time. Therefore, our investment strategies will need to change over time, as well. We cannot look to investment strategies that worked for our grandmothers or even our mothers because the world in which we live is so much different from when they started out on their financial journeys. However, what remains constant are the five stages of investing.

FIVE STAGES OF INVESTING

Let's take a look at these five stages:

1. Select goals for your portfolio.
2. Create an asset allocation for your funds.
3. Understand how to select and build your portfolio.
4. Monitor the ongoing performance of your portfolio.
5. Check to be sure you're tracking against your investment goals in #1.

Stage 1: Goal Selection

Different accounts have different objectives. Your retirement accounts are set up to have a different set of goals from your after-tax accounts. You may have education accounts that are set up to meet educational financing objectives. You have to become clear on what you want to achieve for each type of investment. If you are approaching retirement age and you don't have a significant amount of time to save and invest, your goals may be different from someone who is younger, who does have time to endure swings in the market.

You will need to look at three things when putting together goals for your portfolio:

1. The amount you're starting with
2. The amount you plan to contribute on a consistent basis

3.   The amount of time you have to actually contribute
     to the accounts

To this I'll add a fourth question: When do you need to access
the money? It is not uncommon for people to think that because
they're in their sixties, they need to have a conservative approach. But if you are not going to access the money for ten
years, when you hit your seventies, you can actually be a little bit
more aggressive in your approach. However, if you are going to
be sixty and you need your money by the time you turn sixty-two,
that is cause for a different approach. You will need a different
set of goals for those funds to develop appropriately and a strategic asset allocation for your funds. Which brings me to the
next stage of investing.

Stage 2: Asset Allocation

Knowing what to actually put in your portfolio is a huge part of
helping you achieve your investment goals. Your asset allocation
will be determined by your age and what you're doing to generate income in your career. With that in mind, let's take a look at
how you should be investing your funds based on your age.

I will use the analogy of temperature to describe risk levels.

Level 1: Hot Harvest. Up to age thirty-five, you're going to have a
hot harvest. Hot harvests are more than likely when you're out
of school and have been working for at least ten years. You've got
a great paying job, you are young, and you can pick stocks that
are going to be either in the growth or momentum category,
because you have time in front of you and can assume a little bit
more risk on your portfolio. If you lose, you have time to recover
and bounce back. And most likely, over time, you'll be able to
build up quite a bit of a nest egg. You should take more risks at
this age. You have the ability to make your money work harder
for you because you have your greatest asset, which is time. In

other words, you have more time in front of you than behind you so taking a bigger risk can pay off in the long run. If you're closer to age thirty-five than thirty, obviously you're going to be less aggressive. You will turn the temperature down and have less heat on your portfolio in stocks than you would if you were younger.

Level 2: Lukewarm Risk. The next category, which I call luke-warm risk, concerns investors between the ages of thirty-six and sixty. You're going to be in your prime earning years. You probably have gotten married or are in a long-term partner-ship. You probably own a house and are settled in on the ca-reer you're going to have for the rest of your working life. Because you have more to lose now—a great job, a house, a family—you need to be stable. You still have to take on some risk, but not nearly as much as in your twenties and early thir-ties. You are starting to see the fruits of your labor through savings and investing. What you want to do with your income now is make sure that it gets protected and is still positioned for growth. It will be advantageous for you to look more at growth and value investing and maybe a little bit of momen-tum investing. You may even be able to incorporate dollar cost averaging into your strategy. With dollar cost averaging, you can do a combination of index funds and maybe some individ-ual stocks.

When you get to this lukewarm risk level in your accumula-tion years, you should probably have a nice balance between individual stocks that you select and index as retirement starts to knock on your door.

Level 3: Cold Risk. You're now looking at the age of sixty-one until the end of your life. From age sixty-one until you take the big trip, you probably should be a little on the cold side when it comes to risk. Yes, you no longer have to work for a living. And you cannot afford to take nearly as much risk on your money as you did previously. You need your money to actually be around for you for as long as you live. You do not want to take much risk, if any at all, on your money. Therefore, you do not want to position your money to lose because you most likely won't have the time to make up for any significant losses in your portfolio. At this point, it's all about being able to preserve the capital that you have been able to amass over your working career.

Stage 3: Portfolio Research

The third stage of investing is doing research and selecting the investments that are going to configure or make up your portfolio. Let's take a look at the different types of investments that you can put in your portfolio that will most likely help you reach your financial goals. If we are investing for the long term and for uncertain times (which is all the time), there are two asset classes that will help you reach your investment and financial goals: stocks and bonds.

STOCKS

Stocks have outperformed bonds in the long run. We'll take a closer look at how bonds have done that historically. But with stocks, you know that there's more risk. And as the saying goes, "No risk, no reward." To get a better understanding of the trends, we need to examine historical returns (see figure 2). Stocks have generally returned around 10 percent since 1957. We're not concerned about what happened to stocks in 1957. We need to look at what's happened over the last ten years.[7]

The ten-year cycle average return for the S&P 500 Index is roughly 10 percent. But if we look at the six-year average, it is also about 10 percent. It is safe to say that, over time, stocks can return roughly 10 percent on average. The S&P 500 is a pretty volatile index and has been over the past twenty years. I will add, volatility is not always a bad thing. We need volatility to help us make money in the stock market. With the recent global pandemic, the bull run in the stock market ran even faster, and the S&P 500 (including dividends) closed up around 18 percent.

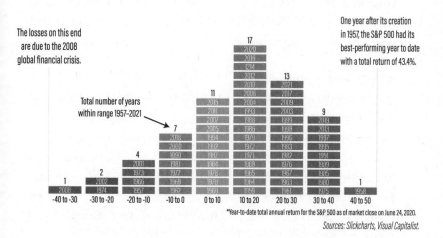

*Year-to-date total annual return for the S&P 500 as of market close on June 24, 2020.

Sources: Slickcharts, Visual Capitalist.

Figure 2

The bull market with stocks has lasted since 2009. Despite a 32 percent correction in March 2020, we saw the fastest rebound from a correction in history. Corrections are going to happen again. We don't know when, but we still have to invest through the uncertainty.

BONDS

Bonds don't get a fair shake compared to stocks. They tend to be boring and not nearly as sexy; however, they should be an important component of your portfolio. The average return for long-term US government bonds is somewhere between 5 to 6 percent. Bonds and interest rates are inversely correlated. This means that when one goes up, the other goes down, and vice versa.

Bonds have never returned over 20 percent in one year. Bond funds have performed extraordinarily well because of the ten-year bond yield performing quite well.

Bonds are great for dollar cost average investors because they provide a consistent, solid return. As a matter of diversification, bonds also offer protection to your portfolio, especially in times where stocks are not performing well.

INVESTMENT TYPES TO ADD TO YOUR PORTFOLIO

So how do you find the portfolio that fits you? Let's take a look at a few different investment strategies that you can utilize to meet your investment goals.

INDEXING

Indexing is an easy, low-cost, low-stress way of being able to invest in a particular stock index, which you can purchase through an exchange traded fund (ETF) or a mutual fund. The most common US index that most investors know of is the S&P 500 Index.

This is known as passive investing, meaning that it's on autopilot. It is the simplest way to build long-term wealth through the stock market. It follows the index where you get to save on fees and you can invest over the long term; however, the amount of money that you put into indexes should be determined based on your age and your investment goals.

To take indexing to another level, you can do something that's called *smart indexing*. Smart indexing allows you to set up your index funds in such a way that no single sector dominates your portfolio. Often, index funds are heavily weighted toward sectors, such as technology, or they can be heavily weighted toward consumer staples. Smart indexing allows you to basically keep your portfolio balanced across all eleven sectors, where no one sector is dominant in your portfolio.

SECTOR FUNDS

This brings me to the next type of fund called "sector" or "specialty" funds. You know how you may like mint chip ice cream or butter pecan? Well, sector funds are similar to choosing ice cream flavors, only you pick a fund that has companies in sectors such as healthcare, technology, or real estate. Sector funds can be a fun way to invest in what you like, but too much of one thing may not be so good for your overall investment strategy. These funds can have huge gains, especially when the sector is hot. But they can be volatile, leaving you with deep investment wounds because most of the companies that make up the fund will move in the same direction, leaving you with little diversification and an increased amount of concentrated risk.

TARGET DATE FUNDS

Another type of investment portfolio that you can use is something called target date funds. Target date funds allow customers or investors to allocate their money into one specific target date in the future. And what will happen with these funds? Say you want to retire in twenty years. Your portfolio will start off with a stock/bond allocation, with a higher percentage heavily skewed to stocks versus bonds. Then, it will shift and become much more conservative, with a higher percentage allocated to bonds. As you begin to get closer to the actual target date of twenty or twenty-five years out, the fund aims to diversify and change the asset allocation over time to minimize the risk of loss on your money. As you move closer to accessing the funds in a target date allocation, your appetite for risk won't be as large as when you were younger. The only drawback with target date funds is that they tend to be more expensive compared to a conventional index, because they are made up of a collection of other funds.

The fourth type of fund is a lifestyle fund. Lifestyle funds really help to meet you where you are as far as your risk tolerance. Lifestyle funds can be invested in based on the type of investor you are. If you are a value investor, you may look for a lifestyle fund that is conservative. If you are looking for something that is a mix of 50 percent bonds, 50 percent stocks, and you want a combination of value and growth, you may get a balanced lifestyle fund.

If you want to have a much more aggressive approach and you consider yourself to be a momentum investor and possibly a growth investor, then you may want to have an aggressive lifestyle fund. These are funds that already come prepackaged for you to invest in based on your desired risks.

Stage 4: Monitor Your Portfolio Performance

Keeping a watchful eye on your prize portfolio will always be your responsibility. It's no one else's job to ensure that you achieve the financial life you desire. With that being said, stay on top of your money. Monitoring your portfolio performance keeps things organized and on track. Let's say that one of your stocks has dropped drastically over the last year or statement period. You can determine if you want to buy more, keep holding, or sell the stock and cut your losses.

When a hundred millionaires were asked, "How often do you monitor/review your portfolio?" over 50 percent indicated "daily" or "several times a day."[8]

Looking at your portfolio or investment balances daily may be overkill, but watching them periodically can help you exhibit the discipline and self-control necessary to get your finances to the level that you desire. If you're not minding your investment business on a regular basis, it's like allowing your child or pet to care for themselves.

Stage 5: Track Against Your Investment Goals from the First Stage

The fifth stage of investing is ongoing monitoring and making sure that you are tracking toward your financial objectives. Ongoing monitoring can be where you select the time of the month or the quarter of the year to review your portfolio and make changes necessary to help you reach your financial goals. Near your birthday is a great time to assess whether or not your portfolio is making progress toward your financial goals. Monthly check-ins would be even better, although just because you check monthly doesn't mean you have to make changes every month. Keep a watchful eye on your investments to make sure those babies are making babies. Knowing how your money is performing puts you in the driver's seat of reaching your financial goals that much faster.

Another piece of advice: don't be like some of my former clients who never opened their statements!

> Start making sure that your investment
> babies are making babies.

In order for you to be able to reach your financial objectives and become a fearless investor, you have to be confident in the information that you look at when it comes to your financial goals. I will go back to mindset and affirmations: if you are afraid to read your statements, you will be afraid to make necessary changes. Remember, the stock market fluctuates over time, and by extension, so will your portfolio. Information is knowledge and it is power.

MAKE A PLAN FOR YOUR PLANS

Finally, when it comes to the five stages of investing, and putting together an investment plan, you need to also build in a margin of safety. What this means is that you give yourself a range of possible outcomes that are acceptable for you. That means if you expect your investment plan will provide $80,000 a year, will you be okay if your investment plan provides $70,000 a year? Will you be okay if your plan only provides $50,000 a year? Is that acceptable?

You have to understand what's going to be your worst-case scenario, and what's going to be your best-case scenario and create a margin of safety, where you have a backup, and then you create a backup to that backup. What this does is allow you to be able to function and carry on with everyday life and give yourself time to course correct, if you need to.

IF YOU CAN'T SEE IT, YOU CAN'T BELIEVE IT, AND YOU CAN'T ACHIEVE IT, RIGHT?

The above statement is a cheeky play on Napoleon Hill's opening quote in *Think and Grow Rich*: "Whatever your mind can conceive and believe, it can achieve." Jokes aside, how do you plan for the things that you can't see? You can't prepare for what you can't imagine, right? Actually . . . you can. What's more, you *should*.

A big mistake that investors make is that they don't just invest for the sake of investing. They seem to always invest with a goal in mind as though they can truly predict what the future holds. Saving money is a necessity and similarly, you must find a way to invest because you won't know the specifics of your financial future.

Another mistake that people make when it comes to money is having just one source of income to fund everyday short-term expenses with no cushion. You need that cushion. You need savings to create the gap between what your expenses are today and what your expenses might be in the future. In short, you should basically prepare by saving for those times in the future, in which you can't possibly even predict or imagine what could happen. It's better to invest knowing things may not go according to plan.

INVESTMENT CLUBS

Have you ever heard the saying "I need new friends"? Or, have you ever been in a situation where you want to talk about money, but your girlfriends don't? Well, back in 2017, I started something called the Stock Sister Circles. These were essentially investment clubs set up by Black women across the country. The whole idea came from many of the women in The Stocks & Stilettos Society, who did not necessarily know how to invest and were a bit timid about putting their money in the stock market.

Going back to chapter 1 where I talked about the importance of surrounding yourself with people who are like-minded, these women did just that. They were all timid (afraid) but they didn't try to talk each other *out* of investing, but rather *into it*. That's the difference.

When I was in my mid-twenties, I was invited to join an investment club. And because of my accounting degree, I was also asked to step up and become its treasurer. There were eight women and two men and we would meet in an office building in downtown Los Angeles to discuss stocks, bonds, and strategies. More importantly, we encouraged each other to educate ourselves on the market and continue to invest.

Unfortunately, I was not able to continue after six months because my job moved me up to Northern California. But that experience of meeting monthly and discussing stocks with people who were like-minded stuck with me for years. When I started The Stocks & Stilettos Society, one of the members in

the Facebook group said, "We should start an investment club."
That suggestion sparked my interest in getting the Stock Sister
Circles off the ground.

What Is an Investment Club?

An investment club is a group of people who come together to
pool money to create a profitable portfolio. At the end of the
day, people come together to make money in the stock market.
Investment clubs have been around since the early 1970s. They
are typically formed as a partnership or as an LLC.

Did you know that there are over thirty-five thousand investment clubs across the country? David Bach's book *Smart Women
Finish Rich* says, according to a 1995 study by the National Association of Investors Corporation (now known as Better Investing), that women's investment clubs outperform men's clubs by
11 percent per year and coed clubs by 5 percent, and did so for
ten of the twelve years included in the study. In fact, the lifetime
earning rate for women's groups was significantly better than
for men, 10.5 percent vs. 9.7 percent. What this says is that
women need to invest together. They need to do it more often
and they will make more money.

Does this mean that you have to ditch your current friends?
No! But what it does mean is that you might want to make some
new friends and become rich together by forming your own investment club. You and your like-minded sister friends are building your own exchange, traded fund, or index, but over time,
being a member of an investment club, you will learn how to
research and evaluate stocks, understand when to add to your
positions, or liquidate stocks.

Most important, you'll create a sisterhood around stock market investing. That's why our investment club program was called
Stock Sister Circles. Investment clubs also provide accountability. You meet monthly and you make consistent contributions.
This ensures that investing doesn't fall by the wayside. If ladies

can meet and do brunch together, then why shouldn't women get together around purchasing stocks?

The Stock Sister Circle program was a huge success. We set up clubs across the country in major cities. Hundreds of women came together to invest in stocks that they might not normally invest in or might not be able to afford on their own. The investment club that I participated in (and am still a member of to this day) is Money Magnets. We started in 2017. The committee who actually got the Stock Sister Circle program off the ground came together as fifteen women contributing just $100 a month and now has built a six-figure portfolio in a little over three years.

We had a virtual celebration—it was such a huge accomplishment. The women of Money Magnets actually reside across six different states and have professional backgrounds ranging from education to engineering to the military. For many of the women, this was their first exposure to the stock market. It is such a fulfilling accomplishment when we all get together annually to celebrate our wins for the year.

So how do you go about establishing an investment club? You need at least three people, but fewer than a hundred. I am confident you know at least three people who can come together and start an investment club.

These are the steps you need to take to get your club up and running:

1. Establish a name and obtain an employer identification number (EIN) so that you can file a tax return for the club. You can get one by filling out the SS-4 form at the IRS website (https://www.irs.gov /pub/irs-pdf/iss4.pdf).
2. Open a brokerage account.
3. Decide on club officers, your monthly meeting date, and your monthly contribution amounts as determined by the club members.

4. Create an investment style for the club. It could mean short-term strategies, buy and hold, and so on.

Be sure to have a plan to have all members participate. Implement an investment literacy plan to ensure that all members are educated on stock market investing.

Investment clubs can be a great way for you to grow your wealth and accelerate your wealth-building activities. Remember, "money loves speed." It's fun in that you do not have to do it alone. We need to bring investment clubs back in style. It's a great way for women to come together and talk about money and feel a safe space to make investment decisions.

This is a great way for you to become a fearless investment club member.

FEARLESS FIGURES
Sylvia Hall

Graduating from law school can easily set you up to walk out with a six-figure bill and a six-month grace period to get on your feet. Throw in Hurricane Katrina and it will force you to take a serious look at your life and finances. This is exactly what happened to Sylvia.

Sylvia graduated from Spelman as an undergrad and earned her JD from Tulane Law just as Hurricane Katrina swept through New Orleans. Forced to evacuate, Sylvia lost most of her possessions. She learned to "pack light" and live a minimalist lifestyle. After things dried up from the hurricane, Sylvia returned to New Orleans, where she crafted a plan to rid herself of student loan debt. Lawyer by day and pizza delivery driver at night, she chipped away at the mountain of debt and saved money to head to Seattle.

Without a job, but with a hope and a prayer, Sylvia worked fearlessly to make it out West. Eventually, she found a job and purchased a condo, which would appreciate in value enough to roll the equity to a larger place. This left her with a rental property and an eagerness to open her own law firm.

Saving money in the midst of life transitions is no small task. But Sylvia became a super saver and invested her money in index funds to meticulously achieve FIRE (Financial Independence Retire Early), where she technically has enough money to cover her living expenses for the rest of her life. "I've found the hardest thing to do is to start. Having high amounts of debt or not being able to see the light at the end of the tunnel can be overwhelming. For me, breaking down big goals into bite-sized chunks gave me the motivation to keep going. Just start."

To do this before the age of forty takes sacrifice, courage, and a willingness to be fearless. Sylvia continues to practice law because she enjoys it and now works to support family and loved ones.

MONEY MOVES

Investing can be scary, but do it anyway. Jump-start your investing journey by following these steps (but grab some coffee first!):

- Write down why you want to invest and what your goals are. Imagine looking through a telescope. Can you see across the street, or can you see across town? Either way, you'll need to build a portfolio to get you to your destination. The same applies to your money. Write down your short-term, mid-term, and long-term goals.
- The Rule of 72 will show you how long it will take to double your money given the rate of return on your investments. Use the formula:

$$72 \: / \: rate \: of \: return$$
$$= years \: to \: double \: your \: money$$

- Let the rule guide you to increase your investment amount (remember, across the street or across town) and the types of investments (how fast you want to get there and risks you're willing to take) you need to look for in an effort to meet your goals.
- Research exchange-traded funds (ETFs), stocks, bonds, and other investments to figure out which one you want to start with.
- Start small and build up your investment muscle as you go. You can always add more money to your investments along the way.
- Watch your balances and make changes when they move away from achieving your investment goals. Losing on an investment can take the fun out of it. Catch your coins before they fall too far and reroute them to another investment slated for recovery. Add money, wash, rinse, and repeat.
- Sit with a financial professional, financial advisor, or Certified Financial Planner (CFP) to help you build your plan and receive guidance as financial markets shift on your way to achieving your goals.
- Many financial institutions have free calculators and planning tools you can use to put together your fearless, million-dollar investment plan. Check out planning tools such as Fidelity's Investment & Planning Tool (https://www.fidelity.com/calculators -tools/planning-guidance-center).

SUCCESS SQUAD

Success leaves clues. Most successful investors are willing to share their investment tips with you. Here are a few people you may be able to rub elbows with to rub your own two nickels together.

Financial Advisor

Advisors at your bank or brokerage generally provide complimentary consultations if you have an account or open an account. They stay ready to answer questions and work with you to build your portfolio, if you're willing to invest the time to meet with them. Check http://aaafainc.com for a directory of African American Financial Advisors in your area.

Financial Planners

Available for a more comprehensive review of your finances, a financial planner will devise a plan to get you started with investing, as well as retirement and college planning. Find a CFP near you at http://letsmakeaplan.org.

Roboadvisors

Half human and half bot, these services allow you to make deposits in a "money machine," and an algorithm goes to work to build your portfolio's balance. Should you choose to accept this option, then be sure you can also meet with a live person to get your questions answered, as humanly as possible.

Friends & Family

Consider starting or joining a club. Learn more about starting your own club at http://betterinvesting.org. The website is a gold mine of information and resources to help you and like-minded people pool resources to get an investment club up and running.

FIVE

Property Pathways

Don't wait to buy real estate.
Buy real estate and wait.

I bought my first house in Stockton, California, when I was thirty-five, and it was definitely a scary time. We had just come out of the Great Recession. A lot of people's stock market portfolios and 401(k)s dropped drastically—by 40 percent, if not more. Buying a house for myself at that time was scary because I didn't know if my job was secure. I was a financial advisor in a large firm and knew from the experiences of my clients and myself that even with the decline in housing values, buying a home was nearly impossible. My income just wasn't high enough to afford Los Angeles prices. But I remembered a couple of things. The first was that this was not my first time actually preparing to buy a house. Before the age of thirty-five, I had three previous opportunities to buy a house, but had gotten so scared that I backed out.

The first time was in Oakland, my hometown. I went to look at a two-bedroom, two-bath condominium near a pretty desirable area of the city and Lake Merritt. This condo was selling for $80,000.

This was around 1996. I viewed the condo and liked what I saw. It needed a little bit of cosmetic work, but for the most part, it was in a secure building, good for me as a new single mother, and it would have been a great purchase at that time. I wanted to make an offer and was ready to make a move on it. I listened to a friend of mine who had gone with me to look at the condominium who said, "You know, if I were you, I wouldn't buy this place as it is. It needs too much work." And just like that, I walked away from the purchase. That was my first opportunity to buy a home for myself and my daughter, which I could have later used as an investment property. In 1997, an $80,000 condominium purchased for someone who had not ever bought a piece of property in her life would've set me up nicely right before a highly profitable housing boom was to sweep through the San Francisco Bay Area. By the way, that two-bedroom condominium is now worth more than $725,000.

The second time I could have purchased a property was in LA. It was a two-story town home in a desirable area and had an attractive listing price of $160,000. I went through the pre-approval process through the Teacher Next Door program, which provided down payment assistance, a low interest rate, and made the homebuying process smooth overall. There was a sticking point for me: I was afraid. I was afraid that I would end up stuck, unable to move if a job opportunity outside of the area presented itself; I was afraid that after my residency term was up (I had to live in the house five years before I could sell it or rent it out) I wouldn't be able to sell it, much less rent it. I was afraid that LA wasn't going to be my permanent home. I was actively considering moving back to Oakland or to my family hometown of Houston, Texas. I focused on all the things the home and homebuying process was not, instead of everything it could have been. And that condo in that neighborhood? Well, the average home price there now is $985,000.

Do you sense a pattern? My fears, largely unfounded, dictated immediate decisions that in the long run would have paid off if I was surrounded by other like-minded people. If I had trusted—no, if I had *affirmed*—what was good about my opportunities instead of what I was scared of.

That brings me to Houston. In 2002, I pulled up my California stakes and moved to my family's hometown. The housing purchase bug had never left me, and upon my arrival, I started looking—casually at first, but my cousin was really pressuring me, but in a loving way. He made it sound so great. If you have ever been to a planned community, there is much to like. After all, everything is new and you get to pick out your own flooring, your cabinets, all of these great customizations that come with a newly constructed home. My cousin and his wife owned a Beazer Home. I was looking at Pulte Homes. I loved so much about the homes, from the large lot sizes, to the square footage, and, of course, all of the possible upgrades. But fear showed up, once again. At this point in my life, I was still figuring out who I was and what I wanted, including if that meant a life in Texas. After all the touring of homes, looking at schools, and planning my new life in Texas, fear and uncertainty took over. I stopped the homebuying process and decided to return to Oakland.

Fast-forward to 2007. I was working as a financial advisor and doing well. I finally found my footing, and because the fourth time's the charm, decided in all seriousness to buy a home. That's when the market imploded. But what made the difference this time was that I didn't have a friend discouraging me from purchasing a home, or a cousin encouraging me. I had a mentor.

I met Michelle in the fall of 1993 at USC's Transfer Day. The Protégé Plus Mentor program was designed for transfers from community college to USC in order to help students make the transition to a four-year school manageable by connecting us to mentors in our field of interest.

Michelle was in her early thirties and she looked like me. She was a bond trader at a large bank. She was confident, fearless, and smart. I immediately gravitated toward her because she was a Black woman doing exactly what I wanted to do. She was an angel who changed my life. I am friends with her to this day.

I finally worked up the courage to buy a home, shook off my fear, and now was pitted against cash buyers, low inventory, and competition from investment groups. My mentor was a person who took me under her wing to support me in my professional life. We spoke by phone and sometimes in person where I shared updates, asked for advice, and remained accountable for goals I had set. In one conversation, she asked me how the homebuying process was going. I shared my frustrations with her and all of the obstacles that seemed insurmountable. I didn't have any more fear, but I definitely didn't seem to have any opportunity. I wanted to live in the city, but I couldn't afford it and I didn't want a long commute if I bought outside the area. My inner nomad considered going back to Texas to buy something, but the distance and another statewide move did not sit well with me. My mentor explained to me that for first-time homebuyers, the most logical and affordable strategy is to buy farther outside the city limits where homes are usually more affordable and plentiful, then after a number of years, take the accumulated equity and use it to purchase a home in the city.

And that's exactly what I decided to do.

The Central Valley city of Stockton, was probably one of the hardest-hit areas in the country during the Great Recession. Not only was there a record number of foreclosures, but the city itself was on the verge of bankruptcy. I knew a bit about the area including that it was a little over an hour's drive north of Oakland, so I decided to visit and look for a housing opportunity. I found a beautiful home listed for $140,000. It was a fixer-upper, and a foreclosure, but that didn't deter me. I had learned my lesson. Real estate has seasons just like the weather. Winter was coming and I knew I had to act. The house had many advantages. I wasn't too far away and I could afford to keep up the payments and the upkeep of the home. I was committed to the house, but not to commuting back and forth from Oakland. The twenty-seven-year-old me would have let all the fear in and kept all of the potential out. I was older now, smarter, and still a little salty about the houses I let get away. I decided to buy the house anyway, so I could actually get in the game and start the clock running on building equity. I had my mother and another family member who needed housing so I moved them in as tenants. The process took approximately thirty days from start to finish. I did it. My goal of holding the keys to a piece of property happened.

Buy land. They're not making any more. In this chapter, I want to walk you through some of the things that worked for me in terms of buying that first home and creating stability for yourself and your family. Buying a home, especially as a single Black woman, can be a launching pad to building wealth. Once you decide you aren't going to let fear rule your life and instead focus on building wealth, your risk tolerance will increase (hello stock market!) and you will realize that the outcome you fear most is a figment of your imagination.

MEET YOUR HOME TEAM

First, get good people around you when buying a home. You might not need a cheerleader per se, but you do need people who are supportive and encouraging of your vision. Remember my advice in chapter 1: you need people you can grow with.

Your "Home Team" also consists of the experts. You need someone who can help you obtain your mortgage at an affordable rate (that's your mortgage broker) and your real estate agent. You can't take these people for granted. These people can make or break you in your transaction to buy your first home. No matter how much you study, no matter how much information you consume, your agent and your mortgage broker are going to be the ones that provide you with financial success. Keep in mind that the homebuying process has two sides: the seller's side and the buyer's side. I am speaking from the buyer's perspective. The seller has their own people and agenda, so getting the right people to represent and assist you is critical.

When it comes to purchasing a home, your mortgage broker is there to help you get the best financing available by finding the best lender. While their motives aren't entirely altruistic, they wouldn't be serving themselves or you if they got you into a mortgage that was too expensive or with unfavorable terms. They want your business (perhaps further down the road you will want to refinance your loan or purchase a second piece of property) and welcome referrals from people you know. You need to make sure you trust this person because they will have access to all your financial information. You also need to feel confident that they will do everything they can to be of assistance—and that includes being responsive to you, as a buyer. Will they return your phone calls and emails in a timely manner? Do they listen to you? Do they ask follow-up questions? Do you feel safe giving them essentially an "all-access" financial pass? These are some questions to consider as you work with your mortgage broker to get the best deal possible.

Opening yourself up financially can be scary because you really have to become vulnerable. Your broker will see how you manage money, how you save money, and based on that information, will determine the amount of home you can afford. Having a conversation across the table from someone you can trust is valuable and underrated. And remember, this person also wants you to be successful.

THE BEST PLACE to start is to have your real estate agent provide you with a couple of referrals of people that they work with. Most likely they work with more than one mortgage person who can help you secure financing. If you have friends who are already homeowners, you can ask them who they worked with and if they come highly recommended. I cannot stress this enough. You want to make sure you work with someone who is very, very trustworthy with your information.

Your real estate agent is really your wingwoman (or -man) on the road to homeownership. They are critical to your overall experience. This person is going to take in all the information, all your wants and desires, and home in on those properties that fit your wish list. I want to be clear that for most first-time home-buyers, your first home is *not* going to be your dream home. As I've stated above, my first house was an hour and twenty minutes outside of the city. Definitely not my dream location, but I had a really nice home that I was able to secure for $140,000. My agent negotiated seller credits, a new roof, and some additional incentives that allowed me to pay just $3,500 for my down payment, including closing costs.

Your real estate agent should be someone who is going to be responsive to you. Since the process involves a lot of moving parts and a lot of financial data, I would suggest that you have someone that you can communicate with at various times during the day who can get back to you in a timely manner, because questions come up all the time and that's going to help quiet the little voices of fear that whisper in your ear. Your agent, like your broker, has a specific goal: sell you a home and broker the financing to make it happen. Your agent makes a commission from the selling price of the home and the mortgage broker gets a commission from the lender who loans you the money. You might be saying to yourself, "Everyone wants to make money off of me!" And that's true. But you have a lot of power because everyone wants to make sure you don't go to someone else to make your homebuying dream come true. Brokers also improve the chances of being approved for financing, especially if you are a first-time homebuyer. For that reason, you want to make sure that the fees you pay for purchasing the home are as low as possible. State this plainly to your agent. Again, your agent wants to be able to help you buy your first home (dream big dreams for yourself, sis!) or help you sell the home you buy so that you can buy another home. If your agent does an outstanding job for you, they know that you will likely refer them to your friends. More friends mean more sales, which means more commissions. To that end, your agent walks a fine line where they are supposed to help keep money in your pocket, while at the same time earning their commission—a percentage of the purchase price of your new home that is paid by the seller's agent. The higher the purchase price, the more the agent gets paid. More money in your pocket leaves you money to make upgrades and, of course, furnish and decorate. That's always the fun part of purchasing a new property. They will negotiate other things on your behalf that you may not even be aware of but that ultimately will benefit you.

I was really surprised during my involvement with heading up The Stocks & Stilettos Society how many women in their forties were not homeowners or did not own some sort of real estate. And when I think back to myself, the first person in my immediate family to purchase property, buying a home in my thirties, it makes me think about all of the fear that comes with buying a house. With a significant purchase, you have hundreds of thousands of dollars potentially on the line that you would be responsible for. I know firsthand how that can be fearful.

I want to help you eliminate that fear and get into a home. Most people will say not to look at a home as an asset. We'll talk a little bit about walking into a home. Obviously, if you have a mortgage, it is a liability. We'll talk about how to set it up as your primary house and then, on the back end, some house hacking tools you can employ to reduce, if not eliminate, your mortgage altogether.

ANOTHER THING IS that sometimes people will give you the idea that renting is better than owning depending on where you are in the country. Some places have high rent with home prices being even higher. That is a realistic barrier to entry, but I really want to impress upon you that if you're looking to grow your wealth and become fearless with your finances, you really have to adopt an entirely new idea of stability when it comes to your home. When you rent, you're typically on a short-term lease. No one rents a house and signs a ten-year lease, right? When you own your own home, you can lock into a stable price that you pay every month, which makes it easier for you to allocate funds to do other things like grow your wealth. Yes, there are some other qualitative reasons for wanting to actually buy a house and that doesn't necessarily mean that you are throwing away money by renting. There are other things that you're throwing away, like peace of mind, knowing that you're going to have to one day move. Renting will have you stressed, losing peace of mind because you're on edge wondering when your rent will go up, especially if you're living in an area that does not have rent control. There is the possibility that you could be asked to move, even if you are in a lease. The owner of the property has move-in rights and may break that lease if they need to live in the property, need to immediately move in a relative, or decide to sell the property. Who wants to live under the assumption that at any time you could be asked to move? This is not an uncommon situation.

Have you said to yourself, "I'm not ready"? Well, I would definitely suggest that you get ready.

What do you have to do to get ready? There are three components that you need to focus on to buy a house: credit, income, and debt.

THREE FACTORS TO CONSIDER WHEN PURCHASING A HOME

Credit

First, you have to make sure that your credit is up to par. This book is not going to discuss what you need to do to raise your credit score. There are several resources on how to do that. What I want to emphasize is that to qualify for a mortgage and a favorable interest rate, you need a credit score above 700 at a minimum. The higher your score, the cheaper it is to borrow money and the lower your mortgage payment will be. Within that credit score range, you're ready to start looking.

Income

The second step is to make sure you have a stable income. You want to be sure that you can afford the house that you want to buy. Affordability is key in looking at your income. You also want to have savings set aside. The biggest component you want to have is at least six to eight months of reserves that would cover all of your housing-related expenses.

There are two components to income. You want to make sure you have money set aside for your down payment. Common wisdom says you want anywhere from 10 to 20 percent as a down payment. I say that because there are programs that will let you put down below 20 percent. If you are self-employed like me, then you will need to provide proof of stable income in one of many ways: you will need at least twelve months of bank statements, as well as profit-and-loss statements (from your most recent tax return). Some banks will require only bank statements for some entrepreneurs, but have all your documents prepared nonetheless. Entrepreneurs will typically have to put down 5 to 20 percent as a down payment and be subject to higher interest rates depending on the lender.

There are also different loan programs available to doctors and lawyers who have significant income, but equally large debt balances.

You want to plan for closing costs and other expenses that may come up after the purchase, items like furniture, decorations, and small repairs as I mentioned earlier. If something unexpected happens like job loss or reduction of hours, you'll have the six to eight months' reserve to fall back on.

Debt

The third step to have in place is your debt. I'm going to say that again. *You want to make sure you have your debt in check.* Your consumer debt should be as low as possible. Common examples of consumer debt include credit cards, student loans, and auto loans. For other types of debt such as medical debt or utility bills, you also need to pay down as much as possible. Student loan debt can help build up your credit if you're making on-time payments, but it's still going to count into your overall expenses when you go to apply for a house.

You want to make sure that all three of these components align when you get your first home. Remember, your first home is not going to be your dream home. So don't get bent out of shape about not moving into something that crosses off everything on your dream home list. Later, you will have everything on your list!

Let's look at the different ways in which you can take the steps it takes to actually buy a home.

WAYS TO PAY FOR A HOUSE

Cash

The first way in which you can buy a house is to pay cash outright. There are situations in which you can buy a property outright for cash. These properties are usually in distressed areas
within and well outside the city limits. The home itself could be
in foreclosure. There might be a tax lien or a tax deed. Homes
that are in probate could also be opportunities to pay cash at
below market rate.

Loan

My recommendation to you is to start off with a loan that you
will be able to more than afford, somewhere in the neighborhood of 25 to 40 percent of your annual gross income. When
you're able to do that on your first home purchase, then that's
going to allow you to at least get in on the property game board.

CONVENTIONAL MORTGAGE

The second way you can buy a home is via a traditional mortgage, also known as a conventional mortgage. Conventional
means that you put down anywhere between 10 to 20 percent
of the purchase price. Typically, conventional loans are issued
by large banks. Large banks have conforming and noncon-
forming loans. When you get a conventional loan through a
bank, they're going to be *conforming*, which means they have to
adhere to certain government standards set by Freddie Mac
and Fannie Mae. These loans are typically issued with the
backing of a solid financial institution, where you could get
favorable pricing with a conventional mortgage. If, in fact, you
put 20 percent down or more, you have the ability to forgo
having to pay private mortgage insurance (PMI). It's not guaranteed. However, in most cases, you can avoid that monthly

cost. And we'll talk about private mortgage insurance in the next section.

FEDERAL HOUSING AUTHORITY (FHA) MORTGAGE

The third strategy to buy a home would be through a Federal Housing Authority (FHA) loan. With an FHA loan, you can put a much lower down payment. FHA loans start with a 3.5 percent down payment, which can make it easier for you to buy a property. But hold on: FHA loans have a sneaky little extra expense called private mortgage insurance (PMI). Private mortgage insurance is where you, the buyer, have to actually pay for insurance for not defaulting on your mortgage. In the rare instance you default on your mortgage, the lender will be fully indemnified for lending you the money. The good news is that your PMI payment goes away when your original mortgage falls to 78 percent of the purchase price.

If you're looking to qualify for a mortgage under the FHA program, the good thing is that it's easier to qualify and you can come in with lower costs out of pocket. The other thing you can do with FHA loans is layer them with down payment assistance programs. It's always great to search the particular city that you want to buy in and see if there are any down payment assistance programs that can help to offset your out-of-pocket costs. These assistance programs may be available for all types of homebuyers, not just first-timers. A first-time homebuyer would be someone who has not purchased property or owned a home within the last three years. Apart from the property itself, FHA is a great way to get started in owning real estate.

VA LOAN

Another way is using Veterans Affairs (VA) loans, if you have served in the military. VA loans are an excellent loan program because they don't require a down payment. If you do have the ability to purchase a home under a VA loan, I would definitely recommend that you go that route because these loan programs have probably the most favorable terms. You do have to apply for eligibility. When approved, you will receive a certificate of eligibility that you can then use to apply for a VA loan.

SELLER FINANCING

The fifth strategy in which you can purchase the home would be seller financing. Seller financing is when you make a private deal with the owner. This person usually owns a property free and clear. The property owner tends to not have a mortgage and you are able to negotiate a purchase price, closing costs, and so on. Seller financing consists of a property owner who is convinced to sell their property by someone who makes an attractive offer, without using a bank to finance the deal. The buyer may or may not be a candidate that can easily qualify for a mortgage with a bank or a lender. With seller financing transactions, you can negotiate to have a much quicker close, with the deal closing in around ten to fourteen days, lowering your out-of-pocket costs. You should be aware that most seller financing deals are a lot shorter in duration than a conventional or traditional mortgage product. You can expect to finance a property over the course of five to ten years, unlike a bank, which can extend up to thirty years. Keep in mind that with these types of loans, there is usually a balloon payment (a large payment) at the end of the loan. Make sure you know what your balloon payment will be, and either prepare to have the cash ready for the payment when it comes due, or be prepared to refinance the loan. Finding seller financing deals can be a lot of work. Word of mouth is a good way to learn about these types of deals. Let real estate agents know you're on the lookout for these types of deals. Anytime you do seller financing, you will need an attorney (ideally a real estate attorney) involved in drawing up the documents, making sure everything is ironclad, and that the seller cannot sell the property out from under you. You want to also make sure that the seller, as well as yourself, can adhere to the negotiated terms. The promissory note that you will sign with the seller will include the interest rate, the repayment terms, as well as any default consequences. You want to make sure that you have your attorney produce the promissory note or evaluate it if the seller's attorney is the one to create the document in a seller financing arrangement. Although you may pay a slightly higher interest rate, this can be offset with other negotiated terms such as a lower down payment or stretching out the terms over a longer period. Most people don't think about approaching a property owner regarding seller financing. But, if you're looking to buy in a buyer's market, seller financing from a motivated seller in a less desirable area may work out in your favor.

Rent-to-Own

A property owner may be willing to work with you if your purchasing profile has a few blemishes. Maybe your debt-to-income ratio is too high or your credit is too weak to strengthen in a short period of time. When you have a rent-to-own agreement, you may also have a potential onetime fee that you pay up front to enter into such an arrangement. Essentially, it's a premium you pay for being able to exercise this option at the end of your lease term. You can expect to pay a little more than market rent because a portion of your monthly rent payment will be allocated to the purchase price. You can look at this as a rent premium that gets allocated toward your down payment on the property. Also, with rent-to-own agreements, you are usually the one responsible for any maintenance or repairs of the property, unlike when you're just renting, and the landlord or owner of the property is the one responsible. In these types of arrangements, you'll have two separate documents: a standard lease agreement and an option purchase contract. There are a couple of ways you can come into the property arena using a rent-to-own option: a rental agreement coupled with a lease option or a lease purchase.

LEASE OPTION

A nontraditional pathway to homeownership can be through a rent-to-own agreement, with an option to buy. This can be an owner-occupied property, or it can even be an investment property. You can get a taste of homeownership if the seller is willing to do a rent-to-own agreement. A rent-to-own agreement, coupled with a lease option, enables you to rent the property for a specified period of time and then, before your lease agreement expires, you have the option to buy the property.

LEASE PURCHASE

Another way to enter the property game and purchase a particular home would be a lease purchase agreement. However, please proceed with caution and be sure to check state and local regulations. Lease purchase agreements can also provide you with the ability to enter into a lease agreement. However, at the end of that lease agreement, you're obligated to purchase the property. You'll definitely want to get a real estate attorney or real estate agent to help you formulate these documents for a lease purchase. The seller may have an attorney create the documents, but have your attorney available to review the documents. For both rent-to-own and lease purchase arrangements, you are going to have to agree on certain things, including the purchase price, which will be at the end of the lease term. With this, you will lock in your purchase price regardless of what's going on in the housing market. You and the prospective seller will negotiate how much of the rent over the lease term will be applied to the principal or allocated toward your down payment. One advantage of a lease purchase agreement is that when you buy the property at the end, you won't have additional moving costs. Another benefit is that you don't have to have a large down payment and get to spread your down payment over the lease term. Also, over the duration of the lease agreement, you can use the time to improve your credit score to secure financing.

However, the main drawback of a lease purchase agreement (versus a rent-to-own agreement with a purchase option) is that, at the end of the lease term, you must purchase that property. Be careful. If you get to the end of your lease agreement and you're unable to secure a mortgage, you may end up forfeiting all the money that you have spent over the course of the lease term. A lease option allows you to walk away with minimal liability, versus a lease purchase where you assume all liability for the purchase. When you enter into a lease purchase agreement, make sure you're able to qualify for a mortgage, or have financial resources available to pay for and secure the property at the end of the lease purchase term.

NEIGHBORHOOD ASSISTANCE CORPORATION OF AMERICA (NACA)

NACA is a program that is designed to help first-time homebuyers. NACA is designed to assist low-to-moderate-income homebuyers. You receive homebuyer education and an assigned counselor who walks you through the homebuying process. Generally, the counselor will work with you to prepare your purchasing profile in the areas of credit, income, and debt. This process can be quite lengthy, spanning upward of one to two years. However, NACA can position you to buy your first home at a significantly reduced interest rate and monthly payment. Is it worth it to go through such a lengthy process? Absolutely. NACA can put you in some of the best mortgage products at some of the most favorable terms for your first home. The program allows you to purchase anything from a single-family home up to a fourplex. I've seen people buy homes valued at $250,000 and pay a mortgage of only $950-a-month that would include property taxes, insurance, as well as their principal and interest payments with a 1.25 percent rate. This program allows you to move into a home where you can actually start to build wealth through homeownership.

ACCELERATED PAYOFF

One common way you can reduce the amount of money that you pay to the bank on a mortgage is to accelerate your payments. Now, I suggest you pay off your mortgage fast, if you can. The interest payments that pile up on a thirty-year mortgage are just not worth the time it takes to pay off the loan. We'll touch on a few strategies to help you reduce your mortgage and/or pay your mortgage off a lot faster. Let's get into it.

An accelerated paydown on an interest-bearing loan translates into less money you'll pay the bank. Remember, banks are in the business of making money. You're in the business of keeping and growing yours—saving you tens of thousands of dollars. You can set up your mortgage so that you can make a biweekly mortgage payment. Using this method, every two weeks, you can pay half of your mortgage at the beginning of the month and half on the fifteenth. Alternatively, you can add an extra monthly payment every year (thirteen instead of twelve payments). Either method will help you reduce the amount of time that it takes you to pay off your mortgage by five years.[1] Instead of a thirty-year mortgage, your house will be paid off in twenty-five years.

WE'VE COVERED A number of ways in which you can squeeze into the property game. Knowing that these programs exist can calm your fear of the process of getting into property and becoming a homeowner. You can begin to accumulate wealth in the form of home equity as a first-generation wealth builder. Somewhere, there is an address with your name written all over it. Don't delay doing what is necessary to get into your home. In order to have fearless finances, you definitely have to become fearless in getting into the property game. Not because you can't afford it, but you have to do the work to put yourself in a position to purchase property. There are so many ways in which you can buy property. You just have to select one method and home in on doing what's necessary: completing the paperwork, paying down debt, improving your credit score, and making sure you can afford the house based on your current income.

HOUSE HACKING STRATEGIES

What if you don't want to live in Timbuktu or have a two-hour commute just to be able to buy a home? There are ways in which you can get your home payment reduced or eliminated *and* possibly generate positive cash flow from your house. House hacking can allow you to cut down on your housing and commute expenses significantly. House hacking is also a way you can afford to pay for an expensive home, using creative ways in which you can get into a home that you desire. House hacking allows you to possibly eliminate such a large down payment, as well. This could come with the ability to move into a larger or multi-unit property, with very little or no money down. Be sure to inquire about this with your real estate agent. With this strategy, you don't necessarily have to start off with a fixer-upper. If you want to buy in the city, but buying in the city or in a highly desirable area comes with a hefty price tag, then this is where house hacking can really come into play. There are a few different strategies in which you can reduce or eliminate your mortgage payment on a month-to-month basis. We will start from probably the most desirable to the least desirable way in which you can house hack.

Purchase a Multiunit Property

What you want to do when house hacking is to provide opportunities for others to to share in the mortgage, if not cover the entire cost or even pay you an amount of profit each month because housing costs are generally our largest living expense. You can buy a multiunit property. It can be a duplex, triplex, or fourplex. The more doors you can get, the better. For example, you can purchase a fourplex that allows you to live in one unit and rent out the other three units that more than cover your monthly mortgage expense. Now, this is easier said than done. You want to make sure that you are buying a multiunit property in an area that has low crime, is close to where you work, or is in a desirable area. This is probably going to be the most desirable house hacking strategy if you are looking to get into the property game. If you can't get a fourplex that you can afford, then you can look at a triplex or a duplex.

Get a More Spacious Home

House hacking can bring additional benefits, especially if you are able to purchase more house, securing a mortgage on a larger home than you initially thought you could afford. With additional space to rent, you can look for homes that have a finished basement. This is key because if you have a home that has a finished basement, then you have the ability to rent that entire space out. Be sure to check with your city's planning department for zoning and permit requirements. If you're able to section off different areas in the basement for bedrooms, living area, and dining area—even better. Do you have a separate entrance? This makes your property prime for a house hacking opportunity. Finished basements that are nice and cozy can set you up to live in the basement, while renting the main house or vice versa. It really depends on what your situation calls for, but this is a great way for you to bring in additional income that can cover your mortgage or a large portion of your mortgage.

Rent Out Rooms or Areas of Your Property

Renting rooms or a garage to college students can actually lower your taxable income, allowing you to write off some of the rental expenses that you have associated with the house. Purchasing in the city can provide you with a short commute or a neighborhood that lends itself to easy access to public transportation, thereby reducing or eliminating transportation and automobile expenses. You may actually buy more of your time back because you're not sitting in traffic fighting the air during a two-hour-long commute to and from work (been there, done that).

I had a friend when I was in college who owned a four-bedroom house. She rented out three of the rooms to college students because her house was near a private college. She was able to rent rooms and have the room rental revenue cover her mortgage. If you have a large enough home, this is a great way for you to house hack and have people who may not need a lot of space pay you rent and get your mortgage paid.

An In-Law or Guest Brings Rental Income

Is there an in-law or a guest house at the back of your primary house? If you have another separate unit that has a kitchen and a bathroom, you can rent that out as a freestanding dwelling. If your property has two structures on it, then you can always rent out the second structure outside of the main home to a college student or a single person to bring in additional revenue. Make sure to run everything by your local government to stay compliant with city ordinances and any permit requirements, where you may be required to attend board hearings, register your dwelling, and notify neighbors, just to name a few.

Consider Short-Term Rentals on Your Home

Another great way in which you can house hack is to rent out your entire space. It's best to check with your city government regarding short-term rental regulations prior to renting for less than thirty days. You may have the opportunity to rent out your home for days, weeks, or months at a time, using platforms like Airbnb or VRBO. You can decide to go this route if you're traveling for work or when you are on extended vacations. Also, converting your house to a short-term rental can help offset the cost of your mortgage payment.

You can also rent out your house on an hourly basis: on apps like Peerspace, for example, clients can rent spaces for photoshoots, meetings, and gatherings. Houses that are spacious and nicely decorated can fetch an additional revenue stream if you rent out your home for corporations to come in and do video shoots, record videos, film commercials, and so forth. If your backyard space allows for entertaining, you can even rent that out to bring in additional income for a backyard soiree. Renting your home out on an hourly basis, where guests don't stay overnight, can add up to a pretty penny, annually.

These are just a handful of ways in which you can actually utilize your home to generate income to help you offset the high cost of housing expenses.

Homeownership is one of the cornerstones to building wealth. To become fearless with finances, it's highly recommended to be in the property game in some form or fashion. There are so many different homebuyer programs, homebuyer courses, mortgage products, and house hacking opportunities for you to be able to afford having a mortgage. This isn't something that is rocket science, and it's absolutely critical that you overcome your fear of homeownership. Sis, get into the property game. Yes, there are rules, regulations, and fees, but by doing your homework (check for permits and the specific requirements your city requires) you can do this! Not only will you learn, but you can do what I am doing right now: teaching you so that you can help someone else in the future. Your future starts now, and the only way you can win at the property game is learning how to play the game and learning how to win at it.

FEARLESS FIGURES
Makeda Smith

Makeda Smith is a multimillion-dollar producer as a licensed real estate broker in the state of Illinois, and the cofounder of Smith & Partners Realty Group, Inc. She is notably known as a real estate growth strategist in her role as CEO of Savvy Chicks in Real Estate, Inc.

Makeda has been practicing real estate in the Chicagoland area for more than fifteen years and shows no signs of slowing down as she takes to social media to aid her burgeoning following of real estate professionals with their social footprint and growth strategy.

With her knowledge and expertise, she has developed a solid relationship with her peers, clients, and local businesses in the area. Her work ethic, integrity, and high level of professionalism has led her to close deals to the tune of over 250 transactions in three consecutive years, earning her the prestigious Top Producer recognition with the Chicago Association of Realtors.

Makeda is well respected not only for her professional track record and integrity but for going above and beyond the call of duty to help women agents grow their social media following, create irresistible content, and generate high converting leads. Makeda is a mother, a wife, and a staple in her community, as she continues to be a fearless trailblazer and trendsetter in the real estate industry.

MONEY MOVES

- Save for a down payment, closing costs, and six to twelve months of reserves.
- Raise your credit score and reduce your debt as much as possible.
- Attend a homeownership seminar. These are often offered through local organizations.

SUCCESS SQUAD

Real Estate Broker

Your chosen real estate broker is there to assist you with preparing to apply for a mortgage, locating a property that meets your needs, and negotiating the purchase price, all while providing insight and strategy to get you the home that you desire. Depending on the state in which you reside, the mortgage broker and the real estate broker may be required to disclose their financial interests. All transactions come with a lot of paperwork. Read every single page and if you are feeling shaky, don't back out, but do get a lawyer to make the legal language plain so you will feel confident signing on the dotted line.

Mortgage Banker/Broker

Financing a property is a huge undertaking and where your mortgage lender comes in as a partner. They are on hand to review your best financing, loan amount, and interest rate options to help you secure the bag that is needed to buy the property.

Real Estate Attorney

A reputable real estate attorney is especially important when you need documents for nontraditional ways to purchase a home. Also, in some states, your situation may need an attorney's assistance. Those states include Connecticut, New York, Massachusetts, Georgia, North and South Carolina, and Delaware.[2]

Accountability Partner

Get an accountability partner to help you stay focused on the goal of homeownership. This could be a friend cheering you to the front steps of your dream home or someone who has successfully gone through the path you intend to take. This helps keep the goal of homeownership at the top of your mind.

SIX

Rock Your Retirement

Freedom is the ultimate retirement hack.

I'm going to say something controversial. I don't like the word *retirement*. Webster's Dictionary defines retirement as "the action or fact of leaving one's job and ceasing to work." It also means giving up work, stopping work. According to Merriam-Webster, retirement is "the withdrawal from one's position or occupation or from one's active working life." A person may also semi-retire by reducing work hours. Many people choose to retire when they are old or incapable of fulfilling their job responsibilities due to health reasons. There's a morbid connotation to the word *retirement*. I like to think of retirement in a more positive light, as part of your life where you get to have full control of your time. Should it take you working twenty-five, thirty, or even forty years to get to freedom from forty-hour workweeks? What if you can put your money in place to help you get to that point sooner?

Retirement can be redefined as the transition from when you are fully dependent on employment income to when you are financially independent, finally. You can make it happen in three years or thirty years—the choice is yours. As with most

employers, upon joining the company and during the onboard-
ing process, a human resources representative will give you a
packet or direct you to a website that has everything you need
to know to enroll in the company's retirement plan. You're pre-
sented with options to have money taken out of your paycheck
before taxes are applied and then you will see a list of investment options. For many, it's comparable to reading Sanskrit—
they have no idea what all of this retirement technobabble even
means.

In this chapter, I want to clear up the confusion, blow up the
whole notion of retirement, and use retirement accounts to your
advantage so you can transition to financial independence—on
your terms. The way in which retirement looked for my grandmother is different from my mother's generation, which will be
different for my generation and even different for my daughter's
generation. According to Morgan Housel in *The Psychology of
Money*, the goal is to become "financially unbreakable."[1] Saving
and investing for retirement puts you in a position to become
financially unbreakable. What if you could reach financial un-
breakability sooner in your life rather than later?

During my grandmother's working years, many workers in
America were provided a pension or a defined benefit program.
They could work for thirty years, forty years, retire with a gold
watch, and receive a guaranteed income from their employer ac-
companied by a Social Security check. During my mother's generation, employees were also provided a pension. However, they
were also given the opportunity to contribute to a defined contribution plan, also known as a 401(k), 403(b), or 457 plan (see figure 3). These are codes that correlate to the federal tax code. In
the early 1990s, we witnessed pensions dying off swiftly with enor-
mous amounts of unfunded liabilities, when corporate raiders
figured out how to skim money off the top from "overfunded"
pensions to finance company acquisitions with large sums of borrowed funds. Today, outside of government pensions, very few, if

any, legacy pensions exist and are offered to newly hired employees. These new employees are left only with the opportunity to invest in a 401(k) plan that the employer may "match." We see that the numbers for Social Security benefits have started to dwindle. Therefore, Millennials may only have a defined contribution plan available to them through their employer and a reduced Social Security check to rely upon.

401(k)/403(b)/457
Personal - Retirement

Trad/Roth/Rollover IRA
Personal - Retirement

Brokerage/Custodial/529
Personal/Joint - Savings & College

SEP IRA/SIMPLE/Solo
Self-Employed - Retirement 401(k)

Figure 3

Let's take a walk down memory lane. The 401(k), which was designed to transfer the liability of saving for retirement from the employer to the employee, was introduced in 1978. I was three years old. Then, the Roth IRA, which allowed you to contribute on an after-tax basis, came into existence in 1998, two years after I received my first job out of college. However, the Roth IRA (which I discussed as a savings tool in chapter 2) was not widely discussed or talked about in corporate America. A paltry 32 percent of Americans have access to these retirement vehicles and actually invest in them. How dare Americans leave the company match, a financial benefit given to them by their employer, on the table! However, studies show that income, age, length of time on your job, and education level contribute to your participation rate in your company-sponsored 401(k) plans. According to Fidelity

Investments, the number of Fidelity 401(k) plans with a balance of $1 million or more jumped to a high of 365,000 in the first quarter of 2021. The number of IRA millionaires increased to 376,000, an all-time high. The total number of retirement millionaires has more than doubled from a year ago. Granted, this is due more to above-average stock market returns after the "Corona Correction" of March 2020 than savings and demonstrates that the stock market will always bounce back, even after a pandemic. I am encouraging you that by dipping your toe in the water you will see it's not so scary. I want you to know that saving and investing for retirement are attainable.

How much should you have saved in your 401(k)? Fidelity Investments recommends, based on your age, that you follow the rules (see also figure 4):

- By age thirty, you should have the equivalent of your salary saved.
- By age forty, you should have three times your salary saved.
- By age fifty, you should have six times your salary saved.
- By age sixty, you should have eight times your salary saved.
- By age sixty-seven, you should have ten times your salary saved.

But if we know we should be saving for retirement, why don't we? Many Americans are not saving for retirement because they simply do not make enough to live off today. Since the 1970s, the cost of living has far outpaced the increase of average workers' income, which makes it very difficult to save. How do we change that? Let's take a look at retirement accounts and how you can best maximize them to provide you with the freedom to finance your lifestyle when you're financially ready—not just when you reach the age of sixty-five.

Retirement Savings Targets

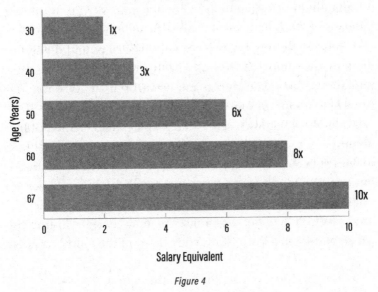

Figure 4

A 401(k), 403(b), and 457 are employer-sponsored retirement accounts that correspond to the IRS tax code. The 401(k) is for companies in the private sector, whereas the 403(b) and 457 were designed for companies in the public and nonprofit sectors. There are other retirement accounts, such as the 401(a), but for this book, we will stick to the three most widely used employer-sponsored retirement accounts. The retirement account tied to an employer, such as a regular 401(k), 403(b), or 457, is not tax-free; it is tax *deferred*—eventually you will pay taxes at a future date when you withdraw the funds. Hypothetically, let's say you have a million dollars in a "forever tax" retirement account. Nearly 30 percent of the balance will go to pay taxes. You have no idea what tax bracket you'll be in, or whether you'll retire by choice or by force. Therefore, anything you withdraw from a 401(k) will be taxable because the money went from your paycheck into your account without giving Uncle Sam his due in taxes.

The best thing you can do with pretax funds in a 401(k) or in a traditional Individual Retirement Account (IRA) is to convert that money into tax-free accounts. Schedule an appointment with yourself to be proactive in taking the steps and doing the work to keep more of your money. If you slip up and let time pass you by, you can expect to pay upwards of 40 percent in the form of taxes for all your hard-earned work and savings.

Ed Slott, well-known retirement expert and certified public accountant, says you want to shift your money from "forever tax" to "never taxed" accounts. By doing so, your retirement distributions become immune from any future tax hikes. However, not everybody is a good candidate for converting "forever tax" accounts to "never tax" accounts. You may consider hitting the pause button on a Roth Conversion if any of the following apply to you:

- *You cannot afford to pay the tax up front*—Switching money from pretax to tax-free will come with a tax bill, including early withdrawal penalties if you're under 59½ years of age.
- *You're in a low tax bracket*—Makes no sense to make this money move and pay taxes on money that may already receive a favorable tax treatment.
- *You will apply for financial aid for your college-bound child*—This can modify the financial aid calculations, and the college will want a larger family and/or personal contribution to Junior's tuition bill.
- *You will withdraw the funds from your retirement account soon*—Earnings are required to remain in the Roth IRA account for at least five years. Any earnings withdrawn prior to this seasoning period will be taxed and early withdrawal penalties may apply if you are under 59½.

A Roth IRA account is a "never tax" account—your tax rate on those funds will always be at zero. Roth IRAs put your money in position to provide insurance against decisions made by Congress regarding taxes. The best thing you can do for your financial future is to convert as much of your pretax money and "forever tax" money as possible into a Roth IRA.

TYPES OF ROTH IRA CONVERSIONS

Being a high-income earner will have you scratching your head to come up with creative, yet legal ways to move money into a Roth IRA. There are three types of Roth IRA conversions and one for every income level:

1. 401(k) to Roth 401(k)
2. Traditional IRA to Roth IRA (Backdoor IRA)
3. 401(k) to Roth IRA (MEGA Backdoor IRA)

Many women, both single and married, find that they are unable to directly contribute to or do a Roth conversion because their modified adjusted gross income exceeds contributory limits. If you fall in that category, then you may consider a *backdoor Roth IRA* contribution. Using this method, you can move money into your Roth IRA to earn tax-free income.

HOW TO CREATE A BACKDOOR ROTH IRA

Here's a step-by-step guide on how to make a backdoor Roth IRA conversion:

1. Put money in a traditional IRA account. You might already have an account, or you might need to open one and fund it.

2. Convert your contribution to a Roth IRA. Your IRA administrator will give you the instructions and paperwork. If you don't already have a Roth IRA, you'll open a new account during the conversion process.

3. Prepare to pay taxes. Only post-tax dollars go into Roth IRAs. If you deduct your traditional IRA contributions and then decide to convert your traditional IRA to a backdoor Roth, you'll need to give that tax deduction back. When it comes time to file your tax return, be prepared to pay income tax on the money you converted to a Roth. And see below for details on the pro rata rule, which plays a big part in determining your tax bill.

4. Prepare to pay taxes on the gains in your traditional IRA. If the money in that traditional IRA has been sitting there awhile and there are investment gains, you'll also owe tax on those gains at tax time.

5. Pay the taxes now and let all the earnings in a Roth IRA account grow tax-free.

BACKDOOR ROTH IRA EXAMPLE

A contribution into a Roth IRA itself produces no tax deduction, and the after-tax portion of the contribution is reported on your tax return. The conversion of that nondeductible IRA is a taxable event, but the portion of the IRA that is attributable to nondeductible contributions is treated as a return of principal and thus has no tax consequences. In the end, this means there will be no deduction for the IRA contribution, and no income from the Roth conversion of that after-tax money, and the net result is a zero impact on your adjusted gross income and a tax liability of $0. This allows you to move the maximum amount allowed by the IRS (as of this writing), $6,000, into a Roth IRA to grow tax-free!

YEAR	NONDEDUCTIBLE IRA CONTRIBUTION*	ROTH IRA CONTRIBUTION	ROTH CONVERSION
1		$6,000	
2	$6,000		
3	$6,500		$12,500
4	$7,000		$7,000
5	$7,500		$7,500

May be a taxable event. Consult with your financial advisor or tax preparer for guidance.

Keep these rules in mind to avoid a 10 percent early withdrawal penalty, if you are under 59½ years old. The conversion needs to be one of the following transfer types:

1. A rollover, where you receive the money from your IRA and deposit it into the Roth within sixty days.
2. A trustee-to-trustee transfer, where the IRA provider sends the money directly to your Roth IRA provider.
3. A "same trustee transfer," where your money goes from the IRA to the Roth at the same financial institution.
4. Be aware of the IRA Aggregation Rule that treats all of your IRAs as one, including any after-tax and pretax contributions that can be distributed on a pro rata basis. Your pretax assets may be subject to tax under IRC Section 408 (d)(2) during a conversion.[2]
5. Avoid making contributions for consecutive years too close together, which can trigger *the step transaction doctrine*, treating both contributions as a single transaction, where you may have to remove funds and be subject to a 6 percent excess tax upon withdrawal.[3]

Not 59½ years old? Then, the IRS allows penalty-free withdrawals for nine reasons, should you need to tap your retirement:

- Unreimbursed medical expenses
- Healthcare premiums while unemployed
- Permanent disability
- Higher education expenses
- Buy, build, or rebuild a home
- Inherited IRA
- Active military duty (for at least 180 days)
- Substantially equal periodic payments[4]
- Pay an IRS levy

One thing about being a fearless retirement investor is not being afraid of what Congress will do when it comes to your retirement in the future. When you set up your accounts to be tax-free, that removes the fear of any tax legislation that Congress can introduce later on in your life—especially in the distribution phase or if you're not able to go back to work.

ROTH IRA: THE RICH WAY

At the end of 2018, approximately 21.6 million taxpayers had Roth IRAs totaling $845 billion, according to the IRS.[5] That equates to an average balance in a Roth IRA of roughly $39,100. Peter Thiel, co-founder of PayPal and venture capitalist, swept across various news outlets when word of his tax-free IRA hit a $5 billion value. So, what is the fearless Roth IRA investment play that Peter Thiel used?

This strategy involved buying a large number of shares in start-ups at a fraction of the cost of a publicly traded company that would be available to everyday retail investors. As those investments increase and provide large gains, you'll be able to have a tax-free retirement vehicle that sets you up for retirement success. Peter Thiel was an accredited investor back in 1990 (more on accredited investors in chapter 9). He made an investment of $1,700 in his Roth IRA account and purchased 1.7 million shares of PayPal in 1999 for

0.001 per share, or $1,700. In three years, Peter Thiel's $1,700 investment soared to $3 billion. By the end of 2019, Peter Thiel's Roth IRA account had reached $5 billion. If he waits until he turns 59½ years of age to withdraw funds, all distributions (including earnings) will be tax-free. Let me repeat: *all of that money will be available to him tax-free.* If he wants to leave it to his beneficiaries, the beneficiaries will also receive the remaining balance in his Roth IRA account nearly tax-free, after accounting for any applicable estate taxes. This is how the wealthy set up their children and their children's children to be wealthy.

Unlike Peter Thiel, we may not get access to startup investing opportunities such as PayPal. With Black women being the fastest growing group of entrepreneurs,[6] it's probably likely that you know a Black woman–owned business who can use a capital infusion. With Black women receiving less than 1 percent of venture capital funding,[7] funds like Backstage Capital, The Fearless Fund, BLXVC, and IFundWomen of Color have sprouted up to provide funding for BIPOC women to grow and scale their businesses. These funds are constantly seeking contributions in exchange for a small piece of equity in a promising startup. You can invest in startups with as little as $250, but you will need to do your research to be sure it's an appropriate investment for you, given the increased risk of failure with startup companies.

BUILD A MEGA BACKDOOR ROTH IRA

Another strategy that you can use is moving money from your 401(k) into a Roth IRA account. This is rarely talked about in financial planning for retirement. But to arm you with this fearless retirement strategy, let's get into it. Yaaassss!!!

You can build tax-free savings over time in your Roth IRA using funds from your 401(k), if your employer-sponsored retirement plan allows you to make nondeductible contributions to your 401(k). You have the ability to convert these nondeductible contributions into your Roth IRA account. You can do this even if your company allows for a Roth 401(k) option. Check with your company to ensure that your company's 401(k) plan allows for in-service withdrawals. That means that as long as you are working with that company, you will be allowed to move the money out, even if you're younger than 59½. Let's take a look at an example.

Say you contribute an additional $25,000 a year as an after-tax nondeductible portion of your 401(k). You can then request an in-service withdrawal and move that $25,000 over into your Roth IRA account. You now have moved $25,000 from your 401(k) into your Roth IRA. Also, if you still meet the income requirements, you can make the annual Roth IRA contribution. As of this writing, you can contribute $6,000 a year to your Roth IRA account—a $25,000 non-deductible contribution plus $6,000 equals $31,000 in Roth IRA contributions for the year. Your Roth IRA funds can work for you and grow tax-free. Shut the front door and go through the back door to keep your money. The good thing is with the Mega Backdoor Roth IRA contribution strategy, there are no income limits stopping you from executing it. If you make a lot of money on your job, you can use this strategy. Be sure to check with the human resources department on the process to initiate a transfer or withdrawal, if necessary.

If you're married and a large portion or all of your income is not necessary to live off of, then you can accelerate your tax-free investment balances, saving a large percentage, if not all, of your income using this Mega Backdoor IRA strategy.

What better way to save for retirement than to save in a Roth IRA account? You can always take out the money you contributed to the Roth IRA. If you recall, if you contribute $100,000 to your Roth IRA, you can take out $100,000 penalty free. Remember, all of your gains must stay in for a minimum of five years and at least until age 59½. Another benefit of funds in a Roth IRA that sweetens the pot is that the IRS does not require you to take minimum distributions at age seventy-two. As a matter of fact, you're not required to take distributions at all. In revisiting Thiel's case, he will not be required to take any required minimum distributions at age seventy-two. He can leave the entire account to his beneficiaries, tax-free.

SELF-EMPLOYMENT AND IRAS

What if you are self-employed and you don't have a company-sponsored 401(k)? You can open a solo 401(k) or you can also use this strategy with a Simplified Employee Pension, or SEP IRA. The only drawback about a Roth IRA, should you grow it to a substantial amount, is that while it may be exempt from individual federal income taxes, it may be subject to state taxes. Should you pass the account down to your beneficiaries, be sure to protect the holdings of your Roth IRA by including it in your estate plan.

One more thing to be mindful of is that anytime you have after-tax funds commingled with tax-deferred funds in any of your retirement accounts, such as a traditional IRA, a SEP IRA, or a simple IRA, you cannot simply convert only the after-tax funds. You have to convert the funds using the pro rata rule for income tax purposes. The pro rata rule states that when determining your tax liability on a conversion from a pre-tax, traditional IRA to a Roth IRA, the IRS will review all of your traditional IRA accounts combined. For instance, if all of your traditional IRAs consist of 80 percent pre tax funds and 20 percent tax-free funds, then that ratio will be applied to your Roth IRA conversion, regardless of the amount of the conversion.

Therefore, you can count on 80 percent of the converted amount to be taxed on your entire IRA balance at the end of the year—not when you conducted the conversion. The IRS is a cold piece of work.

Bottom line, moving money from "forever tax" retirement accounts to "never tax" retirement accounts is best for you and your money in the long run.

FIRE UP YOUR RETIREMENT

What if you could vacation on the Amalfi coast for three months out of the year and not worry about money? Would you like to work out with a Method Man look-alike five days a week while your investments bulk up, too? Or practice self-care while spa-hopping across the country and not have a care in the world when it comes to money?

You're probably saying, "Cassandra! Get out of my head." Well, would you like to have a lifestyle that includes not having to wait until your head is full of gray hair to enjoy life on your terms, where you can do whatever you want to do in your thirties, forties, or fifties—whenever you want?

In financial speak, we call this FIRE (Financial Independence Retire Early).[8] I call it living your best life without a need for money. Crazy concept, right? Simply put, FIRE is not your mother's retirement.

Achieving FIRE doesn't necessarily mean that you'll hand your boss a pink slip. You may love your job, but with FIRE you work because you want to, not because you have to. Did you catch that?

With FIRE, retirement comes early and looks like a treasure chest filled with money wrapped up in an oversized self-care blanket. Achieving FIRE is not for the faint of heart. You will have to mix in an aggressive savings rate, pour in an overdose of discipline to stay the course, and sprinkle in more than a dash of luck that the stock market will give you lots of gains.

Sis, it's not easy. If it were, then everybody would be doing it. You have to be highly motivated and have a plan for how you'll spend all of that free time now that you've made time to go save the world without worrying about your finances.

FIRE Defined

FIRE is when your net worth equals twenty-five times your annual expenses. For example, if your expenses are $100,000 per year, then you can consider yourself on FIRE if you have a net worth of $2.5 million. Even better if this doesn't include your primary residence.

In Fearless Finance speak, when your investment income generates enough passive income to cover your best bougie life, then this girl is on FIRE!

Let's cool down a bit and take a look at a quick example. If you need $100,000 to live comfortably, then you really need $130,000 per year to factor in taxes, because the tax man cometh every year. Therefore, using a conservative annual rate of return of 4 percent, your capital requirement will need to be $3,250,000 to kick off $130,000 in passive income.

$$25 \times annual\ expenses = FIRE$$
$$100,000\ annual\ expenses \times 30\%\ tax\ rate = 130,000$$
$$130,000 \times 1.4\% = 3,250,000\ net\ worth\ goal$$

FIRE Levels

There are levels to FIRE that range from living frugal to living luxurious. With three main FIRE levels, there's sure to be one that may appeal to you, if FIRE is in your peripheral.

- **Fat FIRE:** The most luxurious of them all. Working toward this FIRE level means you're hardly scared and want to live it up in early retirement. Think at least $3 million in net worth.

- **Lean FIRE:** The most frugal out of the three. Freedom is a top priority and you're willing to forgo the expensive handbags, overpriced shoes, and extravagant vacations to live modestly by growing your own food. Think at least $1.25 million in net worth.
- **Barista FIRE:** Named after the baristas at Starbucks, this is a hybrid of Lean and Fat FIRE. You may choose to supplement your passive income by working part-time or taking an extreme payout to work at a job you enjoy and that feeds your soul. Think between one to three million dollars.

In each of these levels, there is one common theme: you're not stressed about money. It's a whole new level of financial wellness.

FIRE is for you if you hate your job or even if you don't. However, you must have a plan that includes a solid financial mindset, aggressive saving and investing, as well as living below your means *before* you leave your job.

Achieving FIRE

You're not scared to throw up the middle finger to your employer and you're ready to work the plan. Here's how to achieve FIRE:

1. *Know your why.* Write down three reasons why you want to achieve FIRE.
2. *Save aggressively.* Your savings rate should range from 20 to 70 percent.
3. *Invest wisely.* Select and build up passive investments such as index funds, ETFs, dividend income, REITs, and physical real estate, to name a few.
4. *Max out your retirement.* Contribute the maximum amount to your pre-tax retirement accounts, such as your 401(k), 403(b), and IRA.

5. *Own your home.* This will lock in your housing cost and neutralize inflation.

Striving for FIRE doesn't have to be full of sacrifices. The greatest sacrifice you'll find is being too fearful to live your best authentic and, of course, financial life.

FEARLESS FIGURES
Gail Perry-Mason

A well-respected authority in the financial industry and a sought-out speaker, Gail has come a long way. From foster care to First Vice President of Investments at Oppenheimer, she continues to preach the retirement and wealth-building gospel to her clients, as well as to youth.

A Detroit native and a single mother, she got a job as a secretary, but realized after watching several people come in who had money to invest that she wanted to learn more about the business. So, she attended night school and earned a degree in finance and financial management services from the University of Detroit (Mercy).

Gail is the coauthor of the national bestselling book *Girl, Make Your Money Grow: A Sister's Guide to Protecting Your Future and Enriching Your Life.* She mentors young women and has encouraged more than a few dozen to become financial advisors.

She's known to be a beacon of light for youth through her community involvement and nonprofit, Money Matters Youth Camp, where she fearlessly teaches core values of financial literacy and awareness. Gail's group of thirty-five aspiring investors was the first youth group to purchase Class B Berkshire Hathaway stock and attend the annual shareholders meeting in Omaha, Nebraska.

Gail has appeared on national outlets such as BET, Fox News, PBS, CNN, MSNBC, CNBC, RadioOne, and NPR Radio. She was a featured financial speaker at the Essence Women's Festival to help spread the word about investing and retirement to more people who look like her.

MONEY MOVES

For the first part of our lives, we do what we have to do. For the second part of our lives, we do what we want to do. During the first part, determine how much is needed to finance the life you plan to live during the second half.

L   List your expenses and determine how much is
    needed to finance your current lifestyle.
I   Invest and grow your savings to cover your expenses.
F   Find additional sources of income and reduce
    expenses to have more money to invest.
E   Educate yourself on Social Security, healthcare, and
    estate planning to protect your investments and
    income.

SUCCESS SQUAD

Retirement readiness requires a money team to help get you started, to hold you accountable, and to assist in preserving your assets along the way. Consider developing a relationship with the following:

Human Resources Representative

They can be a godsend and connect you to the plan provider for your employer. They are often in the know about workplace retirement presentations and resources to help you get started on saving for retirement.

Financial Advisor

This can be someone you trust to give insight and guidance to navigate the financial terrain. They can give you pointers on how to structure your accounts and where to invest your money.

Estate Attorney

They are your go-to for protecting and preserving your fortune. This is important to avoid losing everything you've worked so hard to build.

PART 3

Fearless Fortune

Surplus

Giving activates abundance and you've given yourself a chance to build wealth, fearlessly. You owe it to yourself to be a good steward of what you've worked hard to amass and multiply your money. The final section highlights ways you can accelerate your investments, generate passive income, and move closer to overall financial wellness.

SEVEN

Dividend Income Diva

Invest the principal, eat off of the dividends.

Have you ever been walking down the street and had a $20 bill sitting on the ground that caught your eye? Yeah, me neither. But, if it did happen, then it would put a smile on my face. Well, that's how it is when your stocks pay you in dividends. *Cha-ching!*

There's a famous quote by Warren Buffett that says, "If you don't find a way to make money while you sleep, you will work until you die." Finding money on the street isn't exactly making money in your sleep, but neither way requires any extreme effort on your part. People are drawn to investing in the stock market for the simple fact that you can make money by 1) the stock price increasing from what you initially paid for it and 2) by stocks you own paying you a dividend, or both. Dividends are how companies reward you for being a shareholder. They're the excess profit that companies generate, and then the board of directors will vote to share some of the profit with their shareholders. With dividends, you give yourself a little reward just for investing. How do you actually build a dividend income portfolio and what types of dividends should you be looking for? Hold on, sis. Let me break down this dividend thing for you.

THE ANATOMY OF A DIVIDEND

There are important dates that a dividend investor needs to be aware of. These dates happen in chronological order and determine if you have a dividend coming your way.

The Announcement (or Declaration) Date
This is the date that the company's management will make its next dividend payment. It must be approved by the shareholders before you can get paid.

The Ex-Dividend Date
The ex-dividend date is the most important date of them all. It determines which shareholders will receive the actual dividend payout. If you are a shareholder who actually owns the stock on the ex-dividend date, you can rest assured you will receive the dividend payout, whether or not you actually hold the stock on the payment date. If you are looking to purchase a stock in time to receive the dividend payout, make sure that you actually own the stock on this ex-dividend date. In fact, it is best to purchase the stock at least three business days in advance of the ex-dividend date. If you buy stock after the ex-dividend date, then that company will not show you any dividend love on the upcoming record date.

The Record Date
This is the date that the company establishes to determine whether or not you will receive the dividend on the payment date. The record date is the day after the ex-dividend date. If you purchased stock after the ex-date, you will not be listed in

the shareholder record and thus will not be able to receive a dividend payment.

The Payment Date

This is the day you receive the dividend in your actual account. It can be a week to a month after the record date. Dividends may be paid out in cash, stock shares (known as a dividend reinvestment plan, or DRIP), or, very rarely, in property. Also, your dividends are actually taxed at a much lower rate than your earned income and other forms of W-2 income that you may receive.

DIVIDEND GROWERS

Not all dividends are created equal. There are stocks, and then there are *stocks*, sis. I'm talking about dividend growth stocks, and these should be strongly considered as a part of your Fearless Finances moneymaking machine. Some companies have been issuing and increasing their dividend amount since before I was born, while others have been growing dividends for a fraction of this time. Knowing which dividend stocks to add to your portfolio is half the battle. The other half is knowing when to toss them to the curb. First, we'll take a look at the different categories of dividend growers. Then, we'll talk about the best way to get dividends paid out to you. Since dividends are great little bonuses that can grow over time as you grow your number of shares, the table below illustrates the various types of dividends you can consider for your "This Diva Gets Dividends" portfolio.

DIVIDEND GROWERS			
CATEGORY	NUMBER OF US COMPANIES#	EVALUATION FREQUENCY	CONSECUTIVE DIVIDEND (IN YEARS)
Dividend Kings	38	Annually	>50
Dividend Champions	141	Monthly	>25
Dividend Aristocrats*	64	Annually	>25

DIVIDEND GROWERS (CONTINUED)			
CATEGORY	NUMBER OF US COMPANIES#	EVALUATION FREQUENCY	CONSECUTIVE DIVIDEND (IN YEARS)
Dividend Achievers~	350	Annually	>10
Dividend Contenders	311	Monthly	5–9
Dividend Challengers	284	Monthly	10–24

= listed on the S&P 500 Index | ~ = listed on the NASDAQ
 # = current as of December 31, 2021

DIVIDEND KINGS

Leading the pack on the dividend growers list are the Dividend Kings. Yes, Queen! These companies are the big dogs of the market and are some of the longest-running enterprises around. This group of stocks is considered the most exclusive and is perhaps the most favorable out of all the growers. Dividend Kings are dividend-paying stocks from companies that have had an increase in dividend payouts for at least fifty years in a row. Being able to not only pay a dividend *and* increase the dividend for a company is no walk in the park. As of this writing, only thirty-eight US companies have managed to achieve this regal accomplishment. You may find the full list of Dividend Kings at the Dividend Growth Investor's website (https://www.dividendgrowthinvestor.com/2021/12/dividend-kings-list-for-2022.html). The majority of the Dividend Kings are distributed across two sectors: consumer defensive and industrials. These may seem like two totally nonsexy sectors. But don't be fooled by the bland exterior!

How do you get your hands on Dividend Kings? If you want to own them in a fund, one good fund would be the FT CBOE Vest S&P 500 Dividend Aristocrats Target Income ETF (ticker symbol KNG, unsurprisingly).

All Dividend Kings are also Dividend Aristocrats. However, investing in Dividend Kings may not be a good fit for the portfolio of a young investor. You might say, "Girl, what?!" Yes, because of their established nature, often the low appreciation rates and low dividend yield may leave much to be desired compared to younger companies poised for growth. Young investors should skew their investment dollars toward companies with the potential for double-digit returns. You have more time to make your money work, and the sooner you can do so, the more money your investments will earn over the long term. However, Dividend Kings are good for stable dividend payouts. At the end of the day, Dividend Kings are really good for more seasoned, retired investors because of stability and slight increases in the dividend payout. Also, you may need a large number of shares—think tens of thousands—for the yields and payouts to make sense.

These companies are by no means investment recommendations, but are businesses that have consistently stood the test of at least half a century, withstanding outside economic conditions to provide ever-increasing dividends.

If you had invested an equal amount in the Dividend Kings list starting at the end of 2007, and made updates along the way,

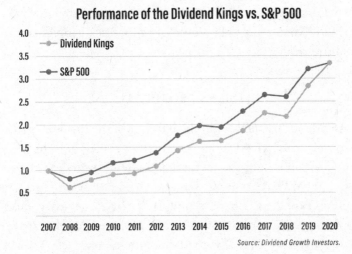

Source: Dividend Growth Investors.

Figure 5

along with rebalancing annually to an equal weighted position, you would have done well. The Dividend Kings list did better than the S&P 500 during this time period, although the Kings did not beat the index every single year. Figure 5 shows the historical performance of the Dividend Kings vs. the S&P 500 since 2007.[1]

DIVIDEND CHAMPIONS

The Dividend Champions are like the little brothers to the Dividend Kings. The Dividend Champions are companies that have consistently increased dividends for over twenty-five years, but fewer than fifty years. The list was originally compiled by David Fish in 2007 and has grown to over 700 companies worldwide, with 129 US companies making the list as of this writing. Again, for a company to consistently grow earnings to be able to boost dividends annually speaks volumes to its stability. The Dividend Champions list includes household names such as AT&T (T) and ExxonMobil (XOM). A full list of the Champions can be found at Sure Dividend (https://www.suredividend.com /dividend-champions-list/). Because of their consistent growth, Dividend Champions make some of the safest dividend stocks for an investor.

DIVIDEND ARISTOCRATS

The Dividend Aristocrats are the darlings of the dividend growers and the most talked about because they consist of companies in the S&P 500 that have increased dividends every year for at least twenty-five years in a row. The Dividend Aristocrats are different from the Dividend Champions in that they are companies that are featured on the S&P 500 Dividend Aristocrats Index (SPDAUDP). The Dividend Champions list casts a much wider net than the Dividend Aristocrats. The S&P 500 Dividend Aristocrats Index, first created back in 1989, is equally weighted and rebalanced every quarter. The number of companies on the Aristocrats listing can range from twenty-six to sixty-five. A full list can be found at *U.S. News & World Report* (https://money .usnews.com/investing/stock-market-news/articles/dividend -stocks-aristocrats).

In order for a company to make this index, it must satisfy the following requirements:

- It must be a member of the S&P 500.
- It has to increase dividends every year for at least twenty-five consecutive years.
- It must meet minimum liquidity requirements.

The Dividend Aristocrats Index tends to actually perform well during bear markets, when the investment environment is kicking off lower returns. But it also pulls its weight in a bull market. The Dividend Aristocrats list is a solid income-growth strategy in which you can make money in your sleep. Growth investing can be such a powerful wealth-generating tool, and the difference in the Dividend Aristocrats list can help you meet that goal. Figure 6 shows the ten-year annual adjusted return of the S&P 500 Dividend Aristocrats Index (as of December 31, 2021).[3]

The companies that make up the Dividend Aristocrats Index boast impressive track records of growth. Aristocrats are required to have a minimum float adjusted market cap of at least $3 billion, and an average of at least $5 million in daily share trading value for the three months prior. The Dividend Aristocrat list is evaluated and updated each year in January. This is where companies can be added or removed based on the requirements. Typically, if a company cuts or suspends its dividend, it can be removed from the index. Dividend Aristocrats

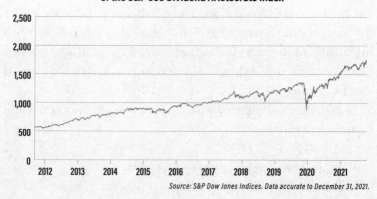

Source: S&P Dow Jones Indices. Data accurate to December 31, 2021.

Figure 6

have increased their dividend payout five times faster than the S&P 500 since early 2014. Dividend Aristocrats are considered the best-in-class dividend growth stocks. Below, you'll find a list of ETFs that track the S&P 500 Dividend Aristocrats Index and various spin-offs, as well.

INDEX	SYMBOL	EXCHANGE TRADED FUND (ETF) THAT TRACKS THIS INDEX	SYMBOL
S&P 500 Dividend Aristocrats Index	SPDAUDP	ProShares S&P 500 Dividend Aristocrats	NOBL
S&P High Yield Dividend Aristocrats	SPHYDA	SPDR® S&P Dividend ETF	SDY
S&P Global Dividend Aristocrats Index	SPGEDAUP	SPDR® S&P® Global Dividend ETF	WDIV
CBOE S&P 500® Dividend Aristocrats Target Income Index	SPATI	FT CBOE Vest S&P 500 Dividend Aristocrats Target Income ETF	KNG

DIVIDEND ACHIEVERS

Dividend Achievers are companies that consistently and regularly increase their dividends to shareholders. The Dividend

Achievers List, a trademarked property owned by NASDAQ, is a collection of over 350 publicly traded companies that have a track record of at least ten straight years of dividend growth. The list is updated annually.

What makes this list so interesting is that many of the companies are probably in a position to make it on the Dividend Aristocrats list. It may be a good idea to get in on these stocks, because today's Dividend Achiever could very well become tomorrow's Dividend Aristocrat stock.

Dividend Achievers have the following requirements:

- They must be incorporated in the United States or its territories.
- They must trade on the New York Stock Exchange, NASDAQ, or the American Stock Exchange.
- They must have increased their annual regular dividend payments for the last ten consecutive years.

Most of the Dividend Achiever stocks actually do not have very high dividend yields, but they can increase yields over time. Since they show a consistent track record of increasing their dividends over the past decade, there are a few indices that you can look at if you want to just buy an index fund that consists of the high-achieving stocks.

For example, the NASDAQ US Dividend Achievers 50 Index (DAY) consists of the top fifty Dividend Achievers whose stocks offer high yields as well as consistent dividends. The US Dividend Achievers Select Index (DVG) contains about two-thirds of the Achievers list, and the US Broad Dividend Achievers Index (DAA) contains the entire list.

In terms of ETFs that track with these indices, Vanguard's Dividend Appreciation ETF (VIG) comes in at a lower cost for your investment compared to Invesco's Dividend Achievers ETF (PFM), because the yield is lower for VIG. Even so, it has a proven track record that has shown attractive investment returns over time. Invesco's High Yield Equity Dividend Achievers ETF (PEY) holds fifty of the highest-yielding stocks on the Dividend Achievers list. Consequently, it has a dividend yield of approximately 4 percent, which is well above the historical yield.

INDEX	SYMBOL	ETF THAT TRACKS THIS INDEX	SYMBOL
NASDAQ International Dividend Select (*Companies with at least 7 years of dividend increases*)	DVGI	Vanguard International Dividend Appreciation ETF	VIGI
NASDAQ US Dividend Achievers 50 (*Top 50 companies from the US Broad Dividend Achievers List*)	DAY	Invesco High Yield Equity Dividend Achievers ETF	PEY
NASDAQ US Dividend Achievers Select (*Select group of 246 companies with at least 10 years of dividend increases*)	DVG	Vanguard Dividend Appreciation ETF	VIG
NASDAQ US Broad Dividend Achievers (*348 companies with at least 10 years of dividend increases*)	DAA	Invesco Dividend Achievers ETF	PFM

DIVIDEND CONTENDERS

Another category of dividends consists of the Dividend Contenders. These companies are all US publicly traded stocks who have increased their dividends for at least ten years, but fewer than twenty-five years in a row. There are over three hundred companies that make up the Dividend Contenders list, including well-known companies such as Home Depot (HD), JPMorgan Chase (JPM), and Mastercard (MC). The Dividend Contenders list can be a good starting point to craft a dividend income portfolio, since many companies on the list provide the best of both worlds: increasing dividend yield and dividend growth. Dividends going up over more than ten years is nothing to sneeze at. These companies are most likely on the path to maintain a competitive advantage, as well as steady earnings and positive future growth in an effort to increase their dividends as they forge ahead.

DIVIDEND CHALLENGERS

Finally, the baby of the bunch and the lesser-known cluster of dividend growers are the Dividend Challengers. They have increased their dividends for the last five to nine years. Many new dividend income investors may dismiss five years of consecutive dividend increases, but don't clutch your pearls just yet. The Dividend Challengers have a strong showing on the dividend growers list due to their providing a dividend where many companies do not. They show the makings of dividend staying power by not cutting or suspending dividends over this time period.

When researching these lists, the Dividend Champions, Contenders, and Challengers list, also known as the CCC list, are grouped together since they do not have to be a part of the S&P 500 Index to be a dividend income grower. These lists are available and updated weekly on such sites as Dividend Radar (www .portfolio-insight.com/dividend-radar) and Seeking Alpha (www.seekingalpha.com).

DIVIDEND SNOWBALL

How do you create your own snowball effect? How do you get to your first $1,000 a month in dividends? Well, let's take a look at how you can actually create your own dividend snowball. Remember from the previous chapter, we talked about how to go from *forever taxed* to *never taxed*? One way to eliminate or avoid taxes on your dividend income would be to create a dividend income strategy within a Roth IRA. Establishing a dividend income strategy inside of a Roth IRA will provide a much more powerful snowball effect on your money. However, if you can't

put it in a Roth IRA account, it's best to do it in a brokerage
account where the tax rate is typically lower on your dividend
income than your earned income from an employer.

To become a successful dividend investor, you need to do a
few things.

- Set income goals
- Set realistic benchmarks
- Identify the stocks you want
- Pick a strategy
- Get that DRIP

Let's review these steps to get you on your way to creating a
passive income stream with dividends.

Step One: Set Income Goals

You need to set dividend income goals. Begin with the end in
mind, by starting with the amount of money you would like to
receive in dividend income per month. This will allow you to
back into the amount that you need to save, as well as the types
of stocks you will need to add to your portfolio based on their
dividend yield and how much your contribution growth rate
must entail. For instance, if you're starting with an initial investment of $1,000 and would like to earn $1,000 per month in
dividends, pick dividend income stocks that have a yield of 4
percent and provide a distribution growth rate of 6 percent. It
will take you twelve-and-a-half years to achieve $1,000 per
month in dividend income. However, if you double your savings
rate to $2,000 a month, you can set up a dividend income port-
folio to provide $1,000 a month of dividend income in just eight
years.

To calculate the amount of money you will need to invest to
achieve a desired amount in dividends, the following formula
will come in handy:

Dividends per month × 12 / Dividend Yield
= Investment Required

Start with $50 per month in dividends and work your way up by purchasing additional shares of stocks in the same dividend paying companies.

Step Two: Set Realistic Benchmarks

Although Step One will help you set goals, in Step Two you want to make sure that you set small intermediary goals first. Your next goal here is to create a dividend income portfolio that will provide you with $50 a month in dividend income. In order to do this, you will need to set up a portfolio of approximately $12,000 that will provide you with $50 a month (or $600 a year). Once you hit that first goal, then you can set a new goal where you now need to hit $100 per month. This would mean you would now have to double your investment to $24,000. And you'll just keep hitting these different benchmarks. That way, you can celebrate the small victories and then set a new goal and celebrate the next victory. This is a great way for you to stay in the dividend income investment game because dividend income investing is a long-term game. You want to give yourself certain milestones to hit along the way so that you stay patient, stay disciplined, and are consistent with your conscience.

Step Three: Identify the Stocks You Want

Identify which dividend stocks you want to have in your portfolio. When deciding which stocks to put into your diversified dividend income portfolio, make sure that you don't only look at stocks that will give you a yield of 4 to 5 percent or better. You want to look for stocks that will also provide capital appreciation on your initial investment dollars. For instance, if you are a younger investor, it's best to look at companies that are on the

Dividend Champions list and the Dividend Challengers list. These companies have had consistent increases in their dividends over the last five to ten years and will provide capital appreciation. As you reach retirement, you may want to set up your dividend income portfolio with stocks from the Dividend Kings and/or the Dividend Aristocrats list, coupled with a few stocks from the Dividend Champions list. As a retired (or close to retired) investor, you are looking for stability and consistency in the dividend increases provided by those companies. You're less concerned about growth, but should be looking more at capital preservation. Therefore, when putting together your dividend income portfolio, it's better to have companies that have gone through a number of economic cycles.

Step Four: Pick a Strategy

Dividend stocks are plentiful and it comes down to stocks you like with generous dividend yields. You've managed to review the list. You've got the Dividend Champions, the Dividend Contenders, and you are trying to decide which stocks to buy. You want to set some criteria for yourself and look at stocks and certain sectors. What you want to do is start off with one to two sectors, and then, once you have hit a certain milestone in that sector, move on to a stock in a new sector. If you don't want to pick stocks, then find an ETF that will provide you with the dividend income goal that you're looking for.

Maybe you want to start off with technology. Find a stock such as Apple in this case that will provide you with a dividend yield of at least 2 percent, or you can find another stock in the technology sector and keep buying shares of the same company. Once you are receiving $50 a month ($150 a quarter) in dividends, then you can move on to the next one.

The other strategy you can use is to pick a small number of companies that would provide you with a dividend every single month. Let's look at a strategy that involves three companies:

- Company A will pay you a dividend in January, April, July, and October.
- Company B will pay you a dividend in February, May, August, and November.
- Company C will pay you in March, June, September, and December.

By purchasing dividend income stocks this way, you'll be sure to receive a dividend every month. You could also add more companies if one company pays you only in June and December. The goal is to ensure that you are receiving some form of dividend income every month.

Once again, make sure that when you are putting together your dividend income portfolio, you try to pick companies that are from different sectors and industries. This is going to allow for diversification across your portfolio, where certain companies can withstand economic cycles.

Step Five: Get That DRIP

When I talk about "DRIP," I don't mean jewelry. DRIP stands for **D**ividend **ReI**nvestment **P**lan. Reinvesting your dividends will help to accelerate your dividend income investment strategy. There are two ways in which you can reinvest the dividends. The first way would be to *automatically reinvest* any dividends that are paid out. You will continue to buy fractional shares of stock and accumulate shares, which will in turn provide you with a higher dividend payout as you go along. The second way will be to actually have your dividends paid out in cash, and then stack the cash until you've saved a certain amount (i.e., $1,000, $2,500, $5,000, etc.). This will allow you to have cash on demand to purchase stocks on the dip. This way, you can buy more shares at a lower price—more shares mean more dividends, which translates to more money for you in the form of a higher dividend payout.

Either of these strategies is fine. Reinvesting dividends using the first method is dollar cost averaging into your dividend reinvestment plan. You're reinvesting dividends simply to increase the number of shares, regardless of price. With the second strategy, you're taking advantage of market downturns—buying low. Not only do you want to increase the number of shares you own, but you want to get them for the lowest price possible. You may not be able to predict where the lowest share price will fall, but getting a stock for 20 to 30 percent below its most recent high is better than buying it at the fifty-two-week high.

If you are closer to retirement or in retirement, another strategy you can use would be to pick companies that are considered the "dogs of the Dow." These are stocks that are typically the highest dividend paying stocks on the Dow Jones Industrial Average. However, their capital appreciation rates tend to underperform the S&P 500 with dogs. With the "dogs of the Dow" strategy, you are going for consistent and increasing dividends without the volatility of high-growth stocks.

DUMPING DIVIDEND STOCKS

Dividend income investing encourages you to pay attention to the fiscal health of a company. Whenever a company cuts or suspends its dividends, you want to look and make sure that this is a temporary condition for the company. Companies that cut or suspend dividends are experiencing trouble and that should be a red flag. At that point, you may want to evaluate whether it makes sense to hold on to the shares, or if you should sell your shares and then purchase shares of another company or more of a company that's performing well in your performance portfolio, in order to continue your dividend income investing strategy. Dividend income investing requires time to work—it's not a get-rich-quick money machine.

Compounding is quite powerful, but with diligence, consistency, growth, and dividend payout increases, you will find that you can become rich later in life. Here is a chart of Warren Buffett's wealth. Warren Buffett started investing at the age of eleven. However, he did not become a billionaire until the age of fifty-six in 1986. It took him forty-five years to become a billionaire. I know you don't have that kind of time. However, you can set up a dividend income portfolio and you can still get rich later in life like Warren Buffett (see figure 7).

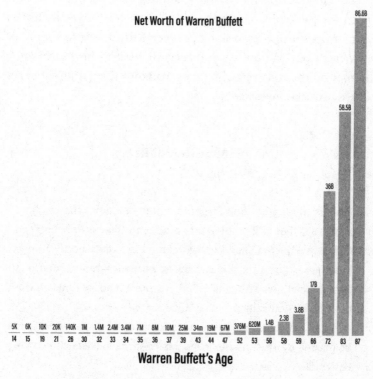

Figure 7

Interestingly enough, Buffett's wealth comes from dividends received on his holdings. However, Buffett's famed Berkshire

Hathaway Class A (BRK.A) & Class B (BRK.B) shares do not pay dividends because Mr. Buffett does not believe it is a good use of cash.[4] Buffett cites double taxation on dividends and instead provides value to shareholders by:

- Reinvesting in existing businesses
- Value-accretion activities
- Stock buybacks

Dividends are last on this list of priorities when it comes to a plan for Berkshire Hathaway's excess cash. With that, Buffett encourages investors looking to receive dividends to simply sell shares to pay themselves a forced dividend, therefore saving money on their tax bill with taxes paid on the earnings in excess of their initial investment.

FEARLESS FIGURES
Robin Watkins

Making history on Wall Street is a huge accomplishment, and Robin did that when she teamed up with Shawn Rochester to launch a $126.5 million IPO, earmarked to help minority-owned businesses and enterprises grow and prosper through mergers and acquisitions with their latest venture—Minority Equality Opportunities Acquisitions, Inc. (MEOA).

MEOA is the first special purpose acquisition company (SPAC) to be headed by African Americans. Ms. Watkins serves as the company's CFO.

"It's Historic and It's Amazing"

MEOA plans to assist Minority Business Enterprises (MBEs) and Black-owned businesses with values of $250 to $500 million to go public. The company plans to target the nearly three hundred

African American, Hispanic, Asian, and Native American MBEs that employ over five hundred people for mergers and acquisitions. Being able to help companies accelerate growth and become publicly traded to raise capital from retail investors is a definite game changer. MEOA plans to keep these as minority-owned businesses after they become public.

Robin is a licensed CPA in Virginia and Maryland, with more than twenty years of government and corporate financial management expertise, as well as a highly regarded financial and operations accountant who graduated from Drexel University. The entrepreneurial spirit runs in her family, with her grandfather owning a trucking company, and her father and other relatives owning businesses, too.

MONEY MOVES

Building a dividend income portfolio for current cash or for reinvestment purposes can seem daunting and overwhelming, at first. Start by selecting five to ten dividend growth stocks for your portfolio. To accelerate the compounding of dividend reinvestment, consider the Global X NASDAQ 100 Covered Call ETF (QYLD) with an average dividend yield of 11.80 percent, or real estate investment trusts (REITS), which are known to pay attractive dividends as frequently as monthly to shareholders.[5]

First, dollar cost average an amount into your dividend income portfolio regularly. You have to keep watering the dividend income growth plant until it is time to eat off the dividends. Set an amount and regular contribution schedule to stay fearless on your quest to build up passive income with this method.

Second, select one of the dividend growers as your starting point to choose companies that consistently increase their dividends, being careful not to trade dividend yield for dividend growth. Don't settle for a small dividend increase, especially if the stock price is not increasing at a reasonable rate either. Be sure to do your research.

Third, buy dividend income stocks when the price is right—buy low, sell high. This gives you an opportunity to buy more shares, thereby increasing the amount you may receive in dividends on those shares.

Fourth, gradually increase the number of dividend income companies that you hold: from five to ten, then ten to twenty and so on. Again, you can decide to own a handful of dividend income stocks and then add in a dividend income ETF to help craft your overall portfolio.

Fifth, turbocharge your dividend income portfolio by not only contributing regularly to your portfolio, but by reinvesting the dividends as well. It's most likely best to accumulate and allocate the dividends that you receive to cash. After reaching a certain amount, as well as buying on the dip, then move to reinvest the dividends into the original company or buy another, more attractive dividend income generating stock.

SUCCESS SQUAD

Building a dividend income portfolio can take time, so grab an accountability partner or set aside time with your financial advisor to build a portfolio that meets your time frame and future income needs.

EIGHT

Real Estate Rock Star

There's no shortage of money, only of people thinking big enough. —Grant Cardone

In December of 2021, I interviewed Angela Yee of *The Breakfast Club* radio show and podcast. In our interview, we talked about what it looks like to actively manage your own retirement. We discussed a wide range of topics, but what stood out most to me was her insistence that her number one priority was that she had a place to live. It seems obvious, but it is very important. If you've never had a secure and stable place to lay your head down at night and wake up in the morning, you know the struggle, fear, and anxiety that that feeling creates. I have had that feeling, so I connected with Angela and understood her need to make sure that the key would always fit in the lock, never to have a landlord push you to leave. I covered homeownership in chapter 5, but what I want to emphasize here is that not only did she secure housing for herself, but her first property purchase was a duplex and the income for the other unit was able to cover a portion of her first mortgage.

Angela Yee stepped into real estate investing on her initial home purchase using that income from her tenant to reduce her mortgage and put money back in her pocket. She bought a second property to cover the cost of her primary residence. That's the investing component of real estate that we're going to dive into in this chapter. Being active to create passive income to underwrite your mortgage or other expenses is spot on.

Although real estate investing really needs its own book, I'm going to discuss a handful of ways that can set you on your real estate investing journey. I'll cover some of the more active ways of real estate investing and then work toward the more passive ways to generate income. Dr. George C. Fraser, CEO of Fraser-Net and founder of the long-running PowerNetworking Conference, said at the annual event, "Buy land, because they're not making any more of it." That's 100 percent actual and factual. As of October 2021, the typical value of US homes reached $312,728, a 19.2 percent increase from October 2020.[1] Between 1999 and 2021, the median price has more than doubled from $111,000 to $269,039.[2]

As a matter of fact, in certain areas of the country, land is selling at a premium. I live in northern California, just outside of San Francisco. Within San Francisco, the typical home value was $1,526,099 as of October 2021, up 8.1 percent from October 2020.[3] Across the country, home prices will continue to rise and people will always need a place to stay. The real estate investing game should be strongly considered as a component of your wealth-building strategy. Fear could be blocking your passive income blessings.

With home values steadily rising and some cities displaying exorbitant barriers to entry, it can be very difficult for the average working person to even get in the real estate investing game. However, it *can* be done—you just have to be creative and strategic about how you enter the real estate investing arena.

Before we jump into the *how* of real estate investing, I want to touch upon the *why* of it. Being fearless with real estate investing creates passive income streams so you can thrive, just like Angela Yee.

FIVE REASONS TO INVEST IN REAL ESTATE

Reason 1: Positive Cash Flow

Monthly income flowing in from tenants or small businesses that pay you rent above your monthly mortgage payment and expenses is positive cash flow—*kaching*! Generating a positive cash flow from your investment property is like turning on a moneymaking machine. Keep in mind that this property does not have to be your full-time job. It could be a side hustle or a supplemental income stream that you use to pay for other important things in your life such as a child's education, to assist with aging parents, or to finance whatever your heart desires. You might use the positive cash flow to save toward an early retirement, take a year off to travel, or work on the novel you have always wanted to write. You get the idea. Creating cash flow from real estate investing can help to supplement or replace income that you earn from your job.

Reason 2: Federal Tax Benefits

The second reason for investing in real estate is for the federal tax benefits. Outside of owning your own business, the tax code is very favorable for those who own real estate investments. If you purchase real estate, you can lower your taxes by being able to claim depreciation on that property. By claiming depreciation on your investment property and deducting expenses associated with the repair and upkeep of the property, you may actually experience a paper loss on your tax return. You may experience a loss on your taxes after owning the property for at least a year, despite your real estate investment property appreciating in value, thereby providing you with positive cash flow.

Reason 3: Leverage

The third benefit of owning and investing in real estate is simply having leverage. By owning an investment property, you may be able to use it as collateral to gain access to additional funding sources to do . . . guess what? Buy more cash-flowing real estate. Leverage is simply being able to use other people's money (or OPM)—in this case, using your real estate to borrow money from the bank. Then, once you get access to OPM, you can use that money to invest in a property that will not only give you back money to repay any borrowed funds, but can create additional positive cash flow on your other investment property. Leverage is a beautiful thing! Because, if structured properly, then you don't put your own money at risk. You're able to use that money from other people to not only pay them back, but to also make money for yourself.

Reason 4: Capital Appreciation

The fourth reason you want to invest in real estate is to have the ability to experience capital appreciation on that real estate property. Over time, real estate property can increase in value. That increase, minus any loans owed against the property, is known as *equity*. Equity is the difference between what you paid for the property at the time and the property's current value according to appraisers. The greater the equity amount is, the more capital appreciation you will experience on the property. You can also do what is called *forced appreciation*. This is where, as the owner of the property, you can do renovations, such as updates to the kitchen and bathrooms. You can even rehab the property by changing the floor plan, adding rooms, or installing new features such as a swimming pool, thereby increasing the value of the property. When you have equity, you have flexibility to make your money work for you with fewer restrictions. You can buy another home, develop a piece of land, or invest in an LLC. The possibilities are endless.

Reason 5: Refinance

Another benefit of owning real estate as an investment is that you can refinance the loan on the existing property. Refinancing a property allows you to pull cash out of the property and use that money toward the purchase of another property. You see where I'm going with this. You can build your real estate investment empire—one refinanced property at a time. The idea is to expand your personal real estate portfolio. The benefit of refinancing a property you already own is that you can take those funds into your next real estate project, tax-free. Finally, with a tenant (or tenants)—depending on what each renter pays versus what you pay monthly on your mortgage—they might be paying most, if not all, of your bill. As you get close to paying off that loan on the property, then it starts to convert to 100 percent cash flow where you create a residual income for yourself in perpetuity, or until you sell, of course.

STRATEGIES FOR REAL ESTATE INVESTMENT

We'll take a look at two broad categories of real estate investment. The first category is *active* investing, where you manage and could very well lay hands on the property. Eventually you can move into *passive* investing, a more hands-off approach. With passive investing, a management company can handle the day-to-day operations for you. You can join a real estate investing group to buy commercial and multiunit residences or allocate funds into a real estate investment trust (REIT).

Active Real Estate
RENTING OUT

One of the most popular ways of active real estate investing is to own the property and rent it out as a landlord. In this scenario, a tenant pays you rent every single month and this becomes a source of income for you.

However, when you are dealing with actual tenants, there are some things you need to be aware of, because they can often be a disadvantage to a landlord. These include repairs, maintenance, and settling disputes or complaints (tenant-to-tenant or tenant-to-landlord). Make sure you have cash reserves to handle any tenant issues ranging from toilets to termites. I remember I had a property with a tenant in it, and we had a situation where the property's plumbing had a main line running through the back of the house and into the other property behind me. That main line went into the street on the other side of the block. There was a massive tree that kept the house cool, but the tree roots were growing into the plumbing, because the pipes were made of clay. The tree roots kept putting pressure on the clay piping and clogged the line, causing frequent backups. I kept a plumber on speed dial because he had to constantly go out to unclog the line. It was beyond frustrating. Eventually I had to get trenchless repair done on the clay piping underground. This cost me $5,000 out of pocket.

It isn't easy being a landlord. Just as you have rights as a landlord, your tenants have rights, too. You would be wise to learn about landlord/tenancy rights in your state so you know what to expect and how to resolve disputes peacefully. Angry or hostile tenants may withhold rent, file complaints against you, or refuse to keep up the property in accordance with your rental or lease agreement. Should you get to the point where you cannot resolve disputes in a fair and equitable manner, it may be necessary to consult an attorney to evict your tenants.

The best advice I can give you is this: choose your renters wisely. Not all money is good money. What's the best type of renter you could approve? What type of renter were you?

- Did you keep your place clean?
- Did you obey noise ordinances?
- Did you pay your rent on time?

This is where your Success Squad can come in handy. Chances are someone in your network already owns a rental property or has dealt with a tenant. Ask them what they love and hate about their tenant and how they would do things differently. What lessons did they learn? A quick conversation with them can provide a shortcut to experience as a landlord. Take this information and craft a checklist of things you desire in a tenant from credit score minimum to maximum number of adults you are willing to allow in the property.

FIX AND FLIP

The second way that you can actively invest in real estate is by way of "fix and flip." We've all seen the shows. A person wants to enter the real estate market and tries their hand at flipping with a contractor or real estate professional. They have a fixed budget, appraisal assessment for the market value of the home, and want to do just enough updating to the property to bring it some razzle dazzle and sell, and pocket the profits. The flipper attempts to make the home "turnkey" ready for the next buyer and walk away with a bag (aka profit). If in fact you're able to get a property below value, then by extension the expense to rehab the property will also be low. Keep in mind that the time of year and location of a property has a lot to do with how much you will pay and what it will cost to rehab. If the market you are in is subject to a tourist season, near the water, or close to festivals, quaint towns, and so on, then expect to pay a premium. This is truer now than ever:

working from home has made living remotely from your place of employment feasible—and for many, attractive.

Let's say, for instance, you find a property that is listed for $200,000, but it needs some cosmetic work done—minor, but manageable changes. It may need a fresh new coat of paint on the interior and exterior. You may have to update the kitchen, bathroom, and maybe change out the windows. You have a budget of $50,000 for all of the cosmetic renovations you would need to have done. With the loan and renovations, you're now looking at a total cash outflow of $250,000. But once you've purchased the home and completed the renovations, this home may now appraise at $375,000. You would then be able to pay off the $200,000 loan and make $125,000 in profit. The $50,000 in rehab costs would be considered a sunk cost, and the $125,000 in profit is subject to taxes since it is a short-term capital gain.

The fix-and-flip game can be very lucrative, but there are a few things to keep in mind. First, research the location. Second, make sure that you keep your costs under control. Third, timing is everything; a quick turnaround is what makes fix-and-flips profitable. Make sure the work in your contract that is to be completed can be done within thirty to sixty days. The longer it takes to complete a project, the longer it might take for you to flip it depending on the market at the time, comparable homes selling in the area, and other factors you may not be able to foresee. Any projects taking longer than sixty days can begin to eat into your potential profit on the resale of the home.

SHORT-TERM RENTALS

The third way that you can actively invest in real estate is going to be through short-term rentals. Starting a short-term rental business (also known as Airbnb or VRBO) allows you to actively invest in real estate and generate income. We live in a society that likes to travel, and services like Airbnb have been able to disrupt the hotel industry by providing more personalized and private accommodations many travelers now want and have come to expect. You can actually be on the rental side of someone that would love to come visit your city, or you can even explore owning or renting out spaces in other, more popular neighboring cities. Airbnb can be quite profitable if you do your due diligence. Also, if you are totally transparent with how you get your property set up for rent with short-term rentals, you have the ability to buy the property outright and use the short-term rental income to effectively pay down the principal on the mortgage. However, not all that glitters is gold. You should definitely investigate if there are city ordinances that limit or prohibit short-term rentals and levy steep operating fees. Cities like Santa Monica, California, have pushed back on Airbnb for a variety of reasons, one of which is lobbying from the hotel industry. Before you jump into renting a room, studio, or your entire home, be sure to read the city's and Airbnb's fine print on restrictions, rights, and responsibilities.

Another option, less peppered with legal red tape, is to start an LLC and then set up a corporate lease structure where you are able to rent out a single-family home, a condominium, town home or an apartment unit—dwellings where the traffic will warrant being able to rent out those units over and above what the monthly rent and expenses would be for leasing that apartment on a monthly basis. Short-term rentals have been a boon in recent years, as people have turned to being able to use other people's properties to basically run their own hotel and hospitality businesses. This is definitely something that you can do to jump-start your real estate investing journey. I suggest that you seek out a course to learn more about Airbnb arbitrage, such as *AirbnProfits* with Kevin Anderson or *Airbnb Automated* on You-Tube. These courses are designed to help you accelerate through the process so that you can avoid some of the many mistakes and pitfalls that come with running a short-term rental real estate investing business.

Passive Real Estate

REAL ESTATE INVESTMENT TRUSTS (REITS)

One of the most widely used forms of passive income real estate investing is through the purchase of real estate investment trusts (REITs). Have you ever pulled up to a Target and then drove across the parking lot to run to the bank? That was most likely part of a REIT you were rolling through. A REIT is a company that owns, and in most cases operates, income-producing real estate. You see, all those stores that have set up shop around Target are paying rent to the REIT. Guess what? That's rental income you didn't really have to work for, outside of investing in the REIT itself. REITs own many types of commercial real estate, including office and apartment buildings, hospitals, senior living facilities, cannabis nurseries, shopping centers, and hotels. Some REITs may even be in the business of financing real estate. REITs can be publicly traded on the NYSE and NASDAQ, publicly registered but nonlisted, or private. The two main types of REITs are equity REITs and mortgage REITs (mREITs). The law providing for REITs was enacted by the US Congress in 1960. The law was intended to provide a real estate investment structure similar to the one that mutual funds provide for investment in stocks. REITs are known among investors for their considerable income because, to avoid incurring liability for federal income tax, REITs generally must pay out an amount equal to at least 90 percent of their taxable income in the form of dividends to shareholders.[4] Sis, that could be you.

REITs can be purchased in your brokerage account or IRA. Very few 401(k) plans have REITs as an investment option, but they can also be purchased outside your employer-sponsored plan. You can start with the Real Estate Select Sector SPDR Fund (XLRE) or the Vanguard Real Estate ETF (VNQ) to dip your toe in the REIT waters.

DELAWARE STATUTORY TRUSTS (DSTS)

Not as well known as REITs, but gaining momentum, is another passive real estate investment called a Delaware Statutory Trust (DST). A DST is another type of investment trust that holds one or more pieces of real property, which investors can purchase ownership interest in, thereby allowing investors to have a fractional ownership percentage in the properties held in the DST's portfolio. Properties in a DST portfolio are generally held for three to ten years. Once a property is sold, the investors receive all sales proceeds, including gains from potential appreciation, which can then be exchanged again to continue deferring tax.

There are several reasons you may want to consider investing in DSTs, including better cash flow and tax deferral benefits.[5] You can invest in DSTs through doing a 1031 exchange or by investing cold, hard cash. It really depends on the requirements of the trust. DSTs are available only to accredited investors.

REAL ESTATE CROWDFUNDING

One passive income real estate investing strategy is looking at online real estate crowdfunding opportunities. Crowdfunding in real estate means that you would start with a minimum investment of around $500. And that $500 is pooled together with other investors who are also looking to enter the real estate investing area with very little skin in the game. These new crowdfunding companies are sprouting up, lowering barriers to entry for investors who thought they did not have enough money to get into real estate investing. Fundrise and Crowdstreet are companies that allow everyday working people to invest in real estate. Investing in crowdfunding companies can allow you to put in very little money and receive residual income over a predetermined time period for your investment. Or you may have a holding period on your funds before you're able to take withdrawals. Online, real estate crowdfunding companies have become more and more popular with new and seasoned investors alike.

SYNDICATES

Another passive real estate investing strategy is something called syndicates. Syndicates are a way for you to invest with friends or other partners. Typically, when you come together and participate in a syndicate, you have the ability to pool money on a much larger scale. A typical initial investment amount can start at $25,000 and go up from there. Syndicates allow you to be a silent partner in a real estate investing group. You make an investment with an investment manager or sponsor, who then sources the properties and deals with the tenants. Then, you sit back and collect a monthly check, based on your ownership percentage less any fees, for having made your investment. These can be quite lucrative, and they allow you to participate in real estate investing without the headache and nightmares that sometimes can come with being a landlord.

There are two types of syndicates: 506(b) and 506(c).[6] The latter are for accredited investors only (more on this in chapter 9). 506(b) syndicates, also known as "friends and family" syndicates, are less stringent with their requirements. You may have an unlimited number of accredited investors and up to thirty-five nonaccredited investors. Syndicates are similar to Black Greek life—you have to be sponsored or invited to become a member of a syndicate. Monick Paul Halm, Esq., of Real Estate Goddesses, and her husband established a syndicate, Vineyard Investment Properties (https://www.vip-assets.com). Together, their syndicate manages more than a thousand "doors" in their real estate portfolio.

Syndicates have become less secretive, more widespread, and feature portfolios of quality properties. Many of the eligibility requirements still require you to be an accredited investor, with an income of at least $250,000 a year or investable assets of over $1 million. Even accredited investors aren't a shoo-in. You still have to know someone who will sponsor you or invite you to join a syndicate.

Again, syndicates are a great way to create passive cash flow from investing in real estate. They allow you to pool money with other investors to purchase properties that you would not normally be able to purchase on your own, such as a neighborhood strip mall with Walmart as the anchor tenant or a three-hundred-unit student housing complex near a college campus. Syndicates can also be set up for you to have part ownership in hotels as well, where you are eligible to receive residual income that is a percentage of profits from room revenue generated from the hotel (see Davonne Reaves's story in the "Fearless Figures" section).

PRIVATE MONEY LENDING

Another passive income real estate investing strategy is through private money financing, also known as hard money lending. This is where you provide the capital used for loans to active investors who "fix and flip" and want to do the heavy lifting, but may not have the capital to see the project to completion. Using a private money or hard money lender is an investing strategy you can use for funds sitting in a savings account to help another investor, one who wants to "fix and flip." In essence, you are able to charge a premium for the use of your funds, earning yourself a higher interest rate than what banks are willing to pay. Say, for instance, you have $100,000 and you're looking to get more than 0.01 percent at the bank. You may be able to take a portion of that and lend it to someone who wants to do a fix-and-flip project by way of a hard money lender. The lender acts as a broker and can position your funds to earn you anywhere from 7 percent to double-digit returns on your money, with the expectation that you will have all of your money returned to you in anywhere from three to twelve months, depending on the length of the project.

One benefit with hard money financing companies (such as Epic Impact Investors, founded by real estate attorney Alexis Hart McDowell) is that there are options available for investors who may want short-term investment opportunities without lifting a hammer. Another benefit is that, typically, hard money lenders do not encumber your funds, locking you into a contract. If you want to be able to take your money out in one to two months, then you're able to do that, as well. Keep in mind, you may not get the full amount of the interest rate that was agreed upon. Be sure to read the fine print on your agreement *prior* to signing, should you want to back out before the completion of the "fix and flip" project. This real estate investing strategy gives you the opportunity to put your money to work for you without having to deal with tenants, termites, and toilets.

TAX LIENS

Another passive income real estate investing strategy is investing in tax liens that have been placed on properties for unpaid taxes to the city or county in which the house is located. Investors can purchase these tax liens via a website or at an auction. Check on the city or county website to find out more information and the dates the auctions are scheduled. Several municipalities use online auction sites, such as Bid4Assets (http://bid4assets.com) to service their auctions. With other auctions, you may be able to actually go to the county courthouse and participate—specifically, sheriff sales and probate sales that deal with fast liquidation of homes; think fire sale. Show up and be ready to present a cashier's check for a minimum required amount, as much as $5,000, in order to join in the bidding process.

Tax liens occur when existing property owners fall substantially behind on paying their property taxes. If the property is free and clear, this gives you an investment opportunity to buy a house that carries no mortgage and pay the amount owed in delinquent taxes. As an investor who is lucky enough to find such a deal, you can purchase a property for a fraction of what the house is worth. Tax liens can differ depending on the state that the property is located in. Not all states offer tax liens. Some states offer tax certificates, where you can pay the back taxes on a property, but the existing property owner may have time to remedy the situation with their taxes, get caught up, and reclaim ownership of the property. Many states that offer tax certificates will institute a set length of time, six to twelve months, that a current homeowner experiencing financial hardship may have to get their property back. If they are unable to pay their taxes on the property by the end of that time frame, then the property will be conveyed to the person who is in possession of the tax certificate.

However, if they do come up with the money to pay their taxes and recover the property before the expiration of the tax certificate, then you are usually paid an attractive interest rate for having purchased the tax certificate to make it worthwhile. Interest rates on tax certificates can be as much as 6 percent. As you can see, the return on a tax certificate can be substantially higher than what your money would earn in a bank. Then there are states, such as California, that have what are called tax deeds should a homeowner become delinquent on their taxes. Tax deeds do not provide a remedy period for the delinquent homeowner to pay any back taxes owed. Once you purchase the tax deed for the delinquent amount in taxes, you assume responsibility and ownership of that particular property. Unfortunately, with a tax deed, the existing property owner loses all rights and possession of the property. Keep in mind that a property owner experiencing financial hardship may not leave the property in a favorable, move-in-ready condition. Be prepared to repair and renovate the property. These are much harder to find along the coastal states, but tax deeds can be an inexpensive way and a low barrier to entry into the real estate investment market. It can be a win-win for you as an investor. Either you'll get the interest if you're holding a tax certificate, the property if the tax certificate expires, or take possession of the property through the purchase of a tax deed.

Real estate investing can come in a lot of different flavors and you have to do your research to determine what flavor works for you. The more you know, the more your pockets will grow. Real estate investing can be as active or as passive as you want it to be. Sis, throw on your "HGTV" hat, and update and decorate a property. Or you can actually just turn over your capital and let other people put your money to work for you, collect your profits, and use those funds to roll over to the next investment opportunity. Then, turn over the profits for you to put in your pocket.

The good thing about real estate investing is that you get to choose how you want to show up in the real estate market, but there is definitely a place for everyone, no matter how much money you have to invest. I don't know who needs to see this, but you should strongly consider adding real estate investing to your wealth-building activities. So become fearless about finding your lane in this game.

FEARLESS FIGURES
Davonne Reaves

What comes to mind when you think about real estate? Hotels, right? Within her first five years of founding The Vonne Group, Davonne became an owner of three hotels totaling more than $30 million.

"For many years I never imagined that I could own a hotel, and now I own three!"

From greeting guests at the front desk to living her ancestors' wildest dreams, this Millennial on the rise and young mother gives birth to new hotel owners and investors through her own hospitality firm. Davonne primarily provides coaching, courses, and ways to raise capital for women of color interested in hotel ownership and investment. Her highly anticipated Future Hotel Owner training program and her forthcoming book, *How to Buy a Hotel: A Roadmap to Hotel Ownership*, represent just a couple of resources to introduce aspiring hotel entrepreneurs to this elusive opportunity.

Her trailblazing initiative to create 221 hotel owners will undoubtedly change the face of hotel ownership for years to come.

Reaves graduated from Georgia State University with a degree in sociology, but got her hospitality chops when she started as a front desk agent at the Hyatt Regency Atlanta. She quickly learned firsthand that only 2 percent of hotel owners are African American and less than 1 percent are Black women.

"Wealth lasts for generations; riches are just for today."

Today, her growing portfolio includes Home2Suites by Hilton in El Reno, Oklahoma, Staybridge Suites Indianapolis-Fishers, and the Hampton Inn & Suites in Scottsburg, Indiana.

MONEY MOVES

- *Fundrise.* Start small with crowdfunding sites such as Fundrise (http://fundrise.com), which is open to accredited and nonaccredited investors. They offer private eREITs for you to invest in, too.
- *Crowdstreet.* Available to accredited investors only. They connect real estate investors to a broad range of debt

and equity real estate investments. You can learn more
at http://crowdstreet.com.

If you're looking at the rental route, you can start with the
following for a property you own:

- Create a rental application form if you don't have one
  already. There are various online templates you can use.
- Check your state's requirements for screening tenants
  (e.g., income, credit score, rental history). There are
  various tools for screening and conducting background
  checks.
- There are software platforms that landlords can use to
  manage maintenance requests, rental payments, and
  complaints.
- Check your community college (or online) to see if
  there are classes on how to create and maintain an
  LLC. The tax considerations are especially important
  to keep in mind.
- Tax liens, deeds, and certificates—there are several
  resources available. Start with the local city or county
  website to learn more about the process.

SUCCESS SQUAD

Get some new friends, those that are like-minded and want to
partner up with you to invest in real estate. As my business coach
would say, the conversation is always different when you sit with
winners. Change your own conversation so you can change the
overall conversation. Talk to your friends and colleagues about
wanting to get into real estate investing. They may be able to
point you in the right direction and connect you with someone
who can give you the 411 on how to get started.

- *Real estate groups.* Join a local real estate group. Several groups are always looking for new members. For short-term rentals, many local groups have started to form such as The Dallas Short-Term Rental Association (http://dallasstra.org). Check to see if there's a comparable association in the city where you want to start a short-term rental business.

- *Real estate brokers and agents.* They always have their ears to the ground about real estate investing opportunities. Be sure you develop a relationship with a few and let them know you're looking to become a real estate investor.

NINE

Aspiring Accredited Investor

Keep going until your bank account
looks like your phone number. —Bossbabes

My first angel investment was for $5,000 in Fresh Bellies, Inc., an organic baby food company where the CEO/ founder is Latina. As a mother, I was excited to see advances made in baby food beyond what was available when I was raising my daughter. The founder was a delight to meet and talk to, as she discussed three distribution channels and her exit strategy for the company. It fueled the flame for my excitement to invest in other Black women– and Brown women–owned businesses. I would go on to invest in:

1. Young Kings, a hair care line for boys
2. HealthInHerHue.com, an online medical directory for women of color

3. Sienna Naturals, a natural hair care line
4. CurlMix, a crowdfunding opportunity in a natural
    hair care brand

Lisha Bell, a friend and founder of the venture fund BLXVC, exposed me to angel investing. With her carefully selected deal flow and my keen review of these companies' financials, I was more than willing to provide support in the way of financial resources for women-owned businesses, which traditionally get 0.006 percent of venture capital backing.

After I started Queens of Capital, an investment mastermind for Black women, many investment opportunities started to flood my inbox—from real estate syndicates to crypto mining rigs. There has been a plethora of ways to make investment money moves. I recently joined forces with a group of Queens, where we have pooled funds to invest in two hotels. Although our investment is relatively small compared to the overall magnitude of the deal, it provided an opportunity for me to invite a few of my gal pals who are unaccredited investors to take advantage of this opportunity. They will most likely become accredited investors in the near future.

In *Money: Master the Game*, Tony Robbins shares how he is an accredited investor, someone who is privy to "special" types of investment opportunities. Well, wouldn't you like to know who qualifies as an accredited investor and how you can become an accredited investor? I'm an accredited investor and you can become one, too. Sis, lean in.

Typically, people invest for a couple of reasons. They invest for retirement or they invest to make a lot of money they can access in the short term. Access to liquid capital is to provide them with financial independence and freedom. With access to enough money or a high enough net worth, you can qualify as an accredited investor.

The Securities and Exchange Commission defines an accredited investor as one who earns significantly more than the average American and whose level of financial sophistication, knowledge, and experience makes them eligible to invest in unregistered securities. An accredited investor must meet one of the following criteria:

1. They earn at least $200,000 a year as an individual or $300,000 as a married couple in each of the past two years and expect to maintain the same income.
2. They have a net worth exceeding $1 million individually or in combination with their spouse, not including the value of their primary residence.
3. They are a general partner, executive officer, or combination thereof for a privately issued fund.

The SEC has recently allowed other individuals to obtain the designation of accredited investor. That would include individuals who hold certain certificates, designations, or credentials, such as Series 7, Series 65, and Series 82 licenses. You can also become an accredited investor if you are a knowledgeable employee of a private fund or an SEC- or state-registered investment advisor. The SEC can add certifications and designations to be included, and encourages the public to submit proposals for other certifications, designations, or credentials. Keep checking back to see if the SEC has expanded the qualifications to become an accredited investor.

In 2020, there were approximately 13,665,475 accredited investor households in the US, representing an estimated 10 percent of all US households. This accounted for $73.3 trillion in wealth. Being considered an accredited investor opens the door to so many more investment opportunities than the average American has access to. This is another place where the great wealth divide happens, where the rich get richer. But the wealthy tend to play on a different playground. An accredited investor may invest in certain types of investments and private issues of stocks that nonaccredited investors cannot invest in.

Let's break down the advantages and disadvantages of being an accredited investor.

Advantages: As an accredited investor, you get access to unique and restricted investments that provide high returns and increased diversification. Accredited investor status gives you a financial advantage over others. Your money makes money at a faster rate.

Disadvantages: The risk of loss is heightened due to the complicated nature of most accredited investment opportunities. In addition to the increased risk, you may have to pay higher minimum investment amounts, higher fees, and your investments may be illiquid.

INVESTMENT OPPORTUNITIES

Accredited investors have access to private equity funds, hedge funds, angel investments, venture capital deals, real estate investment deals, private placement life insurance, and so much more. Let's take a closer look at each of these investment opportunities.

Private Equity

Private equity is capital or ownership of shares in a company that's not publicly traded. Investors raise capital so that they can invest in these private companies for merger and acquisition purposes, or to pursue a new direction for the company. The amount of capital that's invested is often substantial. Accredited investors come into private equity deals as a limited partner. As a limited partner, you receive the income and capital gains that are tied to investing in a private equity fund. Limited partners do not involve themselves in the fund's active management, protecting you from losses beyond your original investment. You can only lose what you put into the actual fund.

Hedge Funds

These are attractive to accredited investors because they employ different investment strategies, primarily with stocks, that are known to provide higher returns for their investors. A hedge fund is designed to provide the highest investment return possible, as quickly as possible. Hedge funds come with hefty fees, charging anywhere from a 15 to 20 percent management fee, if not more, for them to manage your investments in the fund. Although results are not guaranteed, hedge funds appeal to accredited investors because of the high-risk/high-reward component. You will have to make a high initial investment—anywhere from $100,000 up to $1 million—to participate in a hedge fund. Hedge funds can invest in a variety of different securities, including stocks, bonds, commodities, futures, currencies, and derivatives.

Angel Investments

The SEC only allows accredited investors to participate in angel investment groups. Angel investments allow accredited investors to support and invest in newly formed startup companies. You get a seat at the table early on in the growth of a new or rising company. To date we have approximately three hundred thousand Americans who are angel investors. Angel investment groups are popping up across the country. Again, angel investing carries high-risk/high-reward for you if the startup has a promising, yet profitable future ahead of it.

Venture Capital Funds

Venture capital (VC) funds are available to accredited investors who are looking to invest funds in small to medium-sized companies looking to scale. High net worth individuals pool investment funds together to invest in companies, seeking to accelerate the growth of their enterprises and venture capital firms. Think of angel investing, but on a larger scale. Again, VC funds come with very high-risk/high-return opportunities. Most commonly, venture capital funds are directed toward high-tech or emerging industries. Investments in venture capital opportunities are often illiquid until the company actually exits through an IPO merger, acquisition, or—worst-case scenario—goes bankrupt.

Private Placement Life Insurance

Private placement life insurance is an insurance solution designed for accredited investors should you find yourself in a high tax bracket and have large amounts of disposable income ready to invest. Many accredited investors look to private placement life insurance as a tax shielding investment opportunity. There is an insurance wrapper that comes with private placement insurance that allows a high net worth individual to contribute an *unlimited* amount to an investment product. If you're able to invest in this insurance product, then you can later borrow against it and avoid paying taxes on your contributions *and* any gains within the life insurance product. Private placement life insurance is a tactic for accredited investors to cap their tax liability and provide diversification for alternative investments, as opposed to hedge funds, which are highly taxable investments. The tax advantages of private placement life insurance helps to offset what an accredited investor may pay in federal and state capital gains taxes.

Real Estate Investment Deals

Accredited investors are attracted to real estate investment deals where they can become limited partners in high-risk/high-reward real estate deals that put them in the front seat of catching high returns. Accredited investors may also get exposure to partial ownership or investment in hotel chains and other deals as part of a real estate investment syndicate (see chapter 8).

HOW DO YOU BECOME
AN ACCREDITED INVESTOR?

How do you get a leg up and become an accredited investor where you can get access to investment opportunities that are not available to the general public? If the SEC qualifications for becoming an accredited investor don't align with your current financial situation, one of the fastest ways outside of meeting the income or net worth requirements is to take the Series 65 examination and follow all of your state guidelines for becoming an investment advisor. Three to six months' worth of studying to pass this exam can put you in a position to get access to investment opportunities.

Are you a newly minted accredited investor? Start small. Join an angel investment group that allows for investments that can consist of both accredited and nonaccredited investors. Many private investment deals allow for a limited number of nonaccredited investors. In addition to accredited investors, you can network with the right people to get access to those particular deals. The same can be applied to real estate investments. I had the opportunity to invest in a hotel ownership deal with a group of accredited and nonaccredited investors. Minimum investment was $5,000. There are angel investment groups out there that require an investment of as little as $1,000.

On April 5, 2012, President Barack Obama signed the JOBS Act into law. JOBS stands for "Jumpstart Our Business Start-ups." This allows for a broader definition of accredited investor, and it allows retail investors to take advantage of crowdfunding opportunities where they could get in on the ground floor for

investing in startup businesses. This is despite the SEC reporting disclosure requirements for companies that have less than
$1 billion in revenue. It also allows retail investors greater access
to crowdfunding opportunities. It's a great way for you to participate, even as a nonaccredited investor. I had the opportunity
to invest in a crowdfunding opportunity by the Curl Mix and
Natural Hair Care product line created by Kim and Tim Lewis.
Minimum investment was $250 per investor. You have to keep
your ear to the ground on investment opportunities.

According to the Financial Industry Regulatory Authority
(FINRA), another way nonaccredited investors can get in on investment opportunities is under Regulation A (or "Reg A" as it
is known), which allows companies to issue stock without going
through the process of registering with the SEC. A "Reg A" offering
can solicit up to $50 million in securities each year without having
to meet the required registration requirements. To be able to invest as a nonaccredited investor, either your annual income or your
net worth must be less than $107,000 during any twelve-month
period. If so, you have the ability to invest up to the greater of
either $2,200 or 5 percent of the lesser of your annual income or
net worth. If both your annual income and your net worth are
equal to, or more than, $107,000, then during any twelve-month
period, you can invest up to 10 percent of your annual income or
net worth—whichever is less but not to exceed $107,000.[1]

Say your annual income is $150,000 and your net worth is
$80,000. JOBS Act crowdfunding rules allow you to invest the
greater of $2,200 or 5 percent of $80,000 ($4,000) during a
twelve-month period. In this case, you can invest $4,000 over a
twelve-month period.

In summary, the JOBS Act crowdfunding rules allow you to
invest the greater of $2,200 or 5 percent of your income during
a twelve-month period. So if, for example, your income is
$80,000, you would be allowed to invest the greater of $ 2,200
or 5 percent of $80,000, which is equal to $4,000 during the

twelve-month period, since $4,000 is the greater of the two amounts. You can invest $4,000 over a twelve-month period in a startup business. There are several sites, including Kickstarter, that allow nonaccredited investors to get in on investment opportunities for startup companies. This is a great way to introduce yourself to the world of alternative investment opportunities and to accelerate your wealth-building activities.

It is important to emphasize that you should invest money that you can afford to *lose* and you do not need access right away to pay current expenses. Remember, most of these investments are illiquid, meaning you will not have access to the funds for an extended period of time. On average, give yourself anywhere from three to five years to see a return on an investment. Other alternative investments can go out as far as ten years. In summary, becoming a fearless accredited investor can help you reach your financial independence and freedom goals faster.

FEARLESS FIGURES
Lisha Bell

Lisha heads up an angel group of impact investors focused on Black and Latina women, as well as nonbinary femmes, as a co-founder of BLXVC. DealFlow sweeps across her digital desk nearly daily, as she evaluates them to determine which deals to pitch to her network. In Lisha's determination to help underserved individuals, she notes that Black women receive next to nothing for venture funding, and only 1 percent of the wealth in Los Angeles, her hometown, is held by the Black and Latinx communities.

"Where is your money flowing? . . . You've got to be proud of where your money is going," when it comes to angel investing.

Lisha is a tireless advocate of diversity, inclusion, and access. She continues to lead the charge of opening more doors to women in tech and introducing more women of color to angel investing. She has helped to raise tens of millions for startup companies led by women across the country.

Outside of motherhood duties, Lisha also serves as the angel investing coach for The Queens of Capital Investment Mastermind. She was DealFlow Lead at the former Pipeline Angels, former Lead for Pay with Venmo at Braintree (PayPal), and has worked with Wells Fargo, Kohl's, and Feedzai in product management, where she helped to inform a strategic look at payments, fraud, and customer experiences.

Lisha holds a BSc in business administration, information systems from USC, as well as MBAs from UC Berkeley and Columbia Business School.

MONEY MOVES

Visit crowdfunding sites such as Kickstarter.com and WeFunder .com and view the investment opportunities. There are other organizations such as IFundWomen that are always looking for potential investors to financially support women-led business. Surprisingly, your investment can be as little as $250 to $1,000 and can go a long way in helping an entrepreneur live out the mission of her business.

SUCCESS SQUAD

Join a real estate investment group in your area or start your own. Search your alma mater and see if they have a venture capital group that you can become a part of as an alum. You may also add to your LinkedIn profile that you are an aspiring angel investor and join groups such as LevelLeaders.com to learn more about angel investing opportunities.

BONUS CHAPTER

Ten Fears Women Have About Money
and How to Overcome Them

Money is like oxygen for how we go about our everyday lives. It influences our relationship with ourselves and with others, which for many women can create fear and anxiety around our finances. Because of this emotional attachment to finances, even talking about money and managing money can cause women to clam up and become petrified at the thought of it.

In this bonus chapter, I've highlighted the top ten fears women have when it comes to their finances and what you can do to overcome the overwhelm and feel more secure about your money.

FEAR #1:
FEAR OF RUNNING OUT OF MONEY

The most talked-about fear for women is the "Bag Lady Syndrome" and becoming destitute. Even if they've worked hard to achieve a certain level of financial success, many women have the fear of losing it all. It is a well-known fact that women tend to outlive men. According to the US Census Bureau, the life expectancy of a married woman is on average 4.8 years longer than her husband.[1]

Solution: Remember when I mentioned affirmations and the power they have to inspire us and give us a sense of calm to tackle difficult subjects like money? Here's another chance to practice! Our fears are based on what we *believe* is true, not on what is *actually* true. What to do? Grab this fear by the horns! Do not let it win. First, write down what your fear about running out of money looks like. Does it mean a negative account balance? A friend invites you on a Caribbean vacation and you can't afford to go with her? A child needs money for college or other expenses and you can't afford to contribute? You are flat broke when you hit sixty-five? You get the idea.

Then, once you look at this list, face it head-on and make a plan for your money. If there is no plan to tell your money where to go, then your money will go wherever. Doing nothing or putting it off will eventually lead to fear festering to the point where nothing gets done. Break your plan up into three areas to help you get and stay on track to not outlive your money. Your plan should consist of the traffic light method:

- **Red.** These are emergency funds or money set aside to use during a sudden, calamitous event. This could also be money that will remain parked for the long term to grow untouched because you will need these funds in retirement.
- **Yellow.** These are funds used for short-term goals such as vacations or purchasing assets in the near future. Funds in this category are easily accessible to you, but have been earmarked to be used when you need them.
- **Green.** Green means go, and these are funds always at the ready. Passive income streams such as rental income, dividends, Social Security, pensions, and so on, are what make this category of funds easy to come by, after you've put in the work up front to create recurring revenue on the back end for yourself.

At the end of the day, you have to develop a road map for your money or choose to work with a financial professional who can help you put one in place.

FEAR #2:
FEAR OF BEING FIRED

Ouch! Rejection is a hard pill to swallow, but it's even harder when you're not financially prepared to accept walking papers from an employer. When the economy starts to slide into a recession or the entire world is hit with a pandemic, that's when jobs can be put to the test and layoffs ensue.

Solution: Stay ready so you don't have to get ready. Women spend less time in the workforce than our male counterparts because we care for children or elderly parents, which is why we need to become comfortable with the discomfort of asking for more. You have to become more confident in asking for raises to not only get paid your worth, but also to compensate for time away while caring for loved ones. Keep your LinkedIn profile regularly updated and become good at negotiating your salary and raises. Sis, don't be afraid to say it with your chest.

FEAR #3:
FEAR OF NOT SAVING ENOUGH

Your money is often faced with competing priorities, which can make it difficult to know how much to save. More important, it's difficult to know where to save to get the most bang out of every single buck. Most women are risk-averse or very conservative investors and this can backfire when it comes to the compound interest game, which should be played at a higher level. In other words, take advantage of putting your money to work for you by positioning each dollar to make babies and then having each of those babies have their own babies.

Solution: Girl, make your money grow, so you can glow. If only some of your babies are giving birth to new dollars and others aren't, then this is a good time to evaluate where your money may be sitting stagnant and take action to move it where it will grow. Use financial and savings calculators on sites such as Fidelity or MSN Money to begin with the end in mind.[2] By knowing how much you will need to save based on the number of babies you're starting with, how quickly those dollars will give birth to new ones, and the number of dollars you will add over time, you can demystify the amount of money you will need to have more than enough to meet your goals.

FEAR #4:
FEAR OF NOT BEING ABLE TO SUPPORT YOURSELF

Eighty-two percent of women will have to manage the finances on their own as the result of either divorce or death of a significant other or spouse.[3] Married women often carry this fear because a spouse may burn through the financial assets while being cared for, leaving little to nothing for the widow to maintain her lifestyle. Also, with nearly half of all marriages ending in divorce, many women will find themselves alone, managing their own finances, at some point.[4] Women tend to be the least prepared for these life events that require both an emotional and hefty financial transition.

Solution: A layoff, divorce, or death of a loved one can wreak havoc on a woman's financial state. Therefore, it is best to plan for the worst and hope for the best. I remember working with a client who mentioned to me that she wanted to be sure that she had enough money to care for herself should her husband ever leave her. Create your financial plan with a best-case scenario (with you and your spouse's income) and an independent-case scenario (with your income only). Be sure to update this plan every three to five years, based on shifts in your relationship.

Also, death is inevitable and losing a loved one whom you depend on for financial support can leave you making lifestyle adjustments. One way to solve this is having adequate life insurance in place. You want to have at least ten times your household income then add enough to pay off the mortgage and cover any college expenses for the children. If life insurance is unobtainable, then you will need to focus on stacking your savings to get to ten times your income, just to be safe.

FEAR #5:
FEAR OF LOSING YOUR HOME

A home where you have saved and invested thousands of dollars, not to mention a lifetime of memories, can be stripped away in a matter of months. As retirement looms, ensuring there is money for taxes, renovations, and repairs can drain accounts to the point where women are left to flee the nest by force.

Solution: If you fail to plan, then plan to move. If you are considering downsizing, then be sure to count up the costs of moving. Many women opt to move into senior housing communities, which can be as young as a 55+ community, or condominiums where there are amenities provided and included in their housing costs. Dwelling transitions must be a part of your retirement planning conversation and accounted for in your overall retirement plan as you enter your sixties. Packing and moving in your seventies and beyond is not something you should be faced with. Therefore, plan accordingly.

FEAR #6:
FEAR OF BEING SCAMMED

We live in a society where scammers run amok and prey on innocent people who are none the wiser. Women have sent funds overseas and have been swindled out of their life savings after receiving pressure to do so by a fraudulent phone call or letter. People are now being scammed in the digital world through techniques such as phishing—fraudulent emails appearing to be from reputable companies requesting sensitive and personal information. Remember to keep your passwords up to date (and for heaven's sake do *not* use your date of birth, maiden name, or another obvious identifier). Credit card companies and other businesses that collect data will often send an email and a letter about data breaches and you need to read them. These criminals are always looking for a new type of hustle to get all in your financial business and siphon off all your dough. Pay attention to the correspondence you get from companies about your data and privacy rights. If something looks "phishy," be sure to reach out to the company, directly.

Solution: Don't fall for the okey doke. Again, it goes back to taking the time to create a financial plan where you're not left desperate to try anything to make a buck or put under pressure to turn over funds to someone in a faraway distant land, sight unseen. There are laws to protect seniors from financial abuse, and sometimes the culprit can be people and loved ones you already know.[5] They will steal from you and then pretend to help you look for the thief. Be vigilant about protecting your financial information and setting up a plan to tell your money where to go and what to do. Only work with trusted financial professionals from reputable institutions on your financial journey.

FEAR #7:
FEAR OF FINANCES SUFFERING FROM WORK HIATUS

No one likes to be shown the door when it comes to losing a job. It's not only the loss of income, but the loss of workplace relationships with co-workers and an abrupt end to a routine that can leave women in fear of the emptiness that comes with a potential pink slip. All it takes is a global pandemic or a great recession to show that there is no security in job security. These macroeconomic factors make us vulnerable, where we have no control of the outcome that's played on a larger scale.

Solution: In this online game, you always have to play chess and keep your resume and LinkedIn profiles updated. But it is also important to build an emergency fund and create multiple streams of income should you find your main gig is up. Because the employment market is fragile and many employers show little to no loyalty for the contributions you make to their bottom line, it is important to stay connected in this gig economy and find anywhere from one to three additional income streams as a hedge against any looming layoffs. I know I am sounding like a recording on loop, but what would your life look like if you had a work schedule and income according to *your* dreams? I have had jobs that I have loved: great co-workers, companies that respected their employees, and work that had meaning. But that didn't mean I didn't have other dreams and aspirations for myself. Bottom line, even when I loved and appreciated my job, I thought about life after the job ended either by choice or through layoff/downsizing. Because I had this dream, I didn't have fear. This is what I am asking you to do: dream big, without fear but with a plan so if the day comes when you leave your job regardless of circumstance, you are ready with one of the most valuable tools you need, money.

FEAR #8:
FEAR OF BEING A BURDEN

Most women don't like to fathom the idea of becoming a burden on family members. Women will refrain from discussing such delicate matters as who will take care of them when they are unable to care for themselves, out of fear of embarrassment and shame. A woman who finds money confusing and difficult to understand may ignore this financial aspect of her life—jeopardizing her elderly care and leaving it totally up to someone else to manage. She may not want to reveal that she isn't financially prepared, and this may agitate or anger her loved ones. Therefore, she may allow her lack of preparation to fester until her loved ones are left with no choice but to step in and provide care. Many may become a party to the "sandwich" generation, if careful planning is not taken into consideration.[6]

Solution: No one wants to force loved ones to direct financial resources for them. Through proper planning during your younger, healthier years, you can adequately prepare for these expenses in your later years. Be sure to research and gather quotes for healthcare (including supplemental Medicare plans), long-term and final expenses, and life insurance plans before turning sixty years old to minimize your costs as much as possible. It's much better to discuss with your family members what you've managed to put in place for your elder care, as opposed to having tense conversations about what they'll need to support you financially.

FEAR #9:
FEAR OF FINANCIALLY LETTING OTHERS DOWN

Making a bad decision can weigh heavily on just about anybody. But many women fear that they will make a poor financial decision that will lead them to the poorhouse. By our very nature, we as women tend to be risk-averse. We perceive this approach as safe and harmless because we fear losing money. Also, many women have been programmed to be "perfectionists," avoiding being wrong and making mistakes, so as not to come across to others as inadequate or illiterate about how money works.

Solution: We can't afford to take the risk of not taking risks— even when it comes to making decisions regarding money. Maintain a certain threshold of funds in an emergency savings, have a plan, and do ample research before jumping off the ledge when making a financial decision. Also, you can reduce or eliminate this fear by becoming knowledgeable in money matters that will protect your money and communicating with others to help you navigate decisions around money. This can be a trusted advisor or someone close to you that can help bring clarity to a looming financial decision.

FEAR #10:
FEAR OF FINANCIALLY PROVIDING FOR OTHERS

This fear hit home for me as I recently reviewed my cell phone bill where I still cover my twenty-something daughter on my plan. It's not uncommon for "mom guilt" to set in. Women can find themselves financially supporting adult children well beyond a healthy point. Adult children, relatives, and close friends can develop unrealistic expectations or even entitlement issues around your money. This can happen right before our very eyes, especially since, as women, we tend to be natural-born caregivers. If this is you, and as I have just illustrated, it is sometimes me as well, we need to ask ourselves what the deeper reason for supporting able-bodied, capable adults is. I say this because we may feel afraid (see, there's fear again!) that our children, friends, or other adults aren't able to care for themselves without our support. We may be afraid of losing the relationship, or not being "needed" if we cut off access to our funds. We need to set boundaries around how much and when we will support our children and other loved ones. As an example, my daughter has a limit on what she can charge on my cell phone bill. Apps, ringtones, and other "nonessential" charges are not covered by me. She is still in school and as soon as she graduates, she will be responsible for her own bill.

Solution: Repeat after me, "No." Learning how to say no to others allows you to set boundaries that are of a benefit to yourself, and the other person. It puts others on notice to work on becoming self-sufficient and for you to allow others to make decisions based on what is best for them based on the resources they have. Tough love, even when it comes to money, can be quite challenging to deliver. But in the end, it's most likely the best decision for all parties involved. At the end of the day, the best way to combat any fears you may have around money is to equip yourself with the necessary know-how to build confidence. It is also crucial that if you have other people in your circle of trust who have struggled with these issues and successfully managed or overcome them to ask them how they did it. Obviously, reading this book helps, but you also need someone you can call or text, meet for coffee or dinner, have over for a meal, who will speak plainly and honestly about how they dealt with the expectation of financially providing for others. As Black women and People of Color in general, we are more likely to be in this position—especially if you are like me, a first-generation college graduate with a professional degree and income to match. Many of our relatives, and that includes our children, may not yet, or ever, be in this position. I know you feel responsible, but you aren't. You can and should help when and where you can, but be very clear about how much and how long this support will last, and most importantly, why you are helping this person. Get specific. When you have an honest and direct conversation with someone who has been in a similar situation, you can have the confidence and the skill to cut some of the cords that bind you financially to another person.

AFTERWORD

Sitting on the balcony of my newly renovated 1968 condominium, I take in the fresh, cool breeze as I watch the sailboats on the lake drift by. For the first time in a long time, I'm at peace. It's as if every manifestation of the word *home* rests deep in my bones. It all feels like a dream, but it's not. My condo, my lake view, and the hot cup of tea in my hand are all real, the result of hard work—and for most of my life, all I knew was hard work. I reflect for a moment: How did I go from sleeping on an air mattress in my mother's two-bedroom apartment at the age of forty-two to this big-enough-for-me crib in my hometown?

The answer came to me in three words: *I kept going.*

Those nights of writing and planning my next steps in life turned into mornings when the sun started to peek in and the air mattress was nearly deflated. I knew that going out into the real world to get a job wasn't the answer, but I couldn't quite envision the solution. I took inventory of all the things that I enjoyed doing and all the professional experience I had accumulated over the twenty-plus years of my career.

From my first high school job as a part-time file clerk on UC Berkeley's campus to an aspiring broadcast journalist while interning at Fox News 11 in Los Angeles, something had to line up. I tried to disentangle my purpose from my past. That was no easy task. I tried on many career hats in my twenties and thirties. At times, I felt like I was walking in a desert and a mirage would appear. I would head toward the cool lake and palm trees, tempted to rest, only to find out it wasn't real. At other times, I was walking peacefully and a dust storm would come from nowhere, blowing sand in my face. I was discouraged, but

I remembered the words of author and wise healer Iyanla Van-zant: "Everything that happens to you is a reflection of what you believe about yourself. We cannot outperform our level of self-esteem. We cannot draw to ourselves more than we think we are worth."

I reflected on what I thought I was worth. I was smart and talented. I had many roles and responsibilities, and I had no idea how I was going to do them all. I was competent and capa-ble but also insecure. I had doubts about the jobs I held in my life up to that point. Were they pit stops along the way to my destination, or would I be forever sidetracked by discouraging setbacks? Was I worthy of a dynamic career in finance? Of be-coming an entrepreneur who taught women how to handle their own financial futures? Of becoming a millionaire?

Once I made the declaration that I was worthy of a peaceful, prosperous, and abundant life, I shook off all the dust I had been collecting over the years and did what I and so many Black women have done: snap my fingers and tap my toes to a few bars of Beyonce's song "Diva" and make my next move.

If I was going to be world-class at anything, including my purpose, I had to keep going. And I did. One day in the fall of 2016, I pulled up to one of my favorite pit stops, Starbucks, and had a meeting on my cell phone with my former mentor Paul Carrick Brunson. I remember sitting in the parking lot being excited and deflated at the same time. My new business wasn't gaining any traction. I would make live appearances on Peri-scope (a once-popular livestreaming service) to educate and inform the three to five people who tuned in to watch me. A handful of times it was only me and one of my friends on the app. But I kept going. I knew that this meeting scheduled with Paul had to count. The call started with me firing off my plans to teach women how to invest in the stock market. I had all these innovative ideas on how I was going to deliver instruction and

Paul stopped me dead in my tracks with a game-changing response: "Choose one."

I took his advice. I slowed down, looked at my list of plans, and picked the one I was most enthusiastic about. I went on to launch a self-paced home study kit, *The Stock Starter Kit*, that would end up in the hands of thousands of women who wanted to learn how to invest in the stock market and remove the fear factor. While these little boxes full of investing know-how were being shipped and opened at homes across the globe, things were changing in my own home. I was excited that word was spreading about The Stocks & Stilettos Society, but the enormity of my sacrifices quickly became apparent.

Taking time away from my significant other to write one more email. Stepping away in the middle of my niece's birthday party to do a virtual speaking engagement on a Sunday. Skimping on my workouts only to have my fibroids balloon to the point where I appeared to have a little bun in the oven. I thought these were all necessary sacrifices on a personal level so that I could preach the gospel of financial freedom. I thought they would not be in vain because of the sheer amount of work that needed to be done to change the financial trajectory of women's financial lives. I was fortunate to witness so many women winning and feeling good about themselves and what they were able to accomplish. Besides, to whom much is given, much is also required, right?

I had to learn the hard way: if I didn't take care of myself, then I wouldn't be able to take care of others. I had to reset by establishing boundaries in order to enjoy life while I'm able. I drink plenty of water and I exercise. I get on the phone and laugh with my girlfriends. I put my phone in silent mode when I want to sleep or just unplug and rest. My daughter and I have a warm and nurturing relationship, and I have been fortunate enough to see her grow and spend quality time with her. I even dust off my stilettos and go on dates. I am so proud of myself. Every job I have ever had prepared me for the work I am doing today. The people I have met, the women I have mentored and coached, the cities I have traveled to, the jobs that I didn't get, the jobs that I did get, the houses I didn't buy—all of it culminates into this moment. Every time I put the key into the lock of my condo, I smile. Every time a woman in one of my investment groups sends me a thank-you message for changing her life, I smile. Nothing worth doing is ever easy, but affirmations of gratitude and a willingness to listen to good advice, believe in yourself, and promise yourself to never quit will make the hard road a bit softer.

I've come a long way from the little girl that grew up on welfare in West Oakland, aka The Lower Bottoms. By the time this book comes out, I'll be on my way to being fine, fifty, and nothing short of *fearless*.

ACKNOWLEDGMENTS

I am my ancestors' wildest dreams, but it inevitably takes team-work to make the dream work. So many have contributed to my life that has brought me to this very place, as an author.

First of all, I give thanks to God. Second, I would like to thank my mother, Deborah Carruthers, who has been a constant and stable force in my life, as well as my late father, Robert Cummings, who embedded drive and tenacity in me from the gate. Without these two, there would be no me.

I would like to thank my sisters Deanisha, Robin, Sarah, Latisha, Simone, and Roshonda for being a beacon of light. Your smiles coupled with laughter will always warm my heart. However, I have to give a special thanks to my sister LaKysha, who has been my personal advisor, substitute therapist, relationship counselor, and part-time life stylist. Thank you for always being honest and truthful even when you knew it would agitate my spirit. I will always be appreciative of the late-night, early-morning phone calls.

Many thanks to the Mathews—Harold, Roz, and Jenaya—for just being there. My life would look so different had you not been a part of it.

Success is contagious and I've been truly blessed to have been mentored by some amazing human beings. Angela Perry, thank you for being my first mentor and for giving me my first crack at financial advisement. I got a front-row seat at what it looked like to be a powerhouse woman from USC to AIG. Thank you for opening your heart and home to me, as well as showing me how to handle myself with grace and femininity in a room full of men.

Speaking of men, thank you to the men in my life that have mentored me on this journey. Paul Carrick Brunson, thanks for imparting your intelligence that gave way to the entrepreneurial prowess in me. You truly showed me how to do good in this world and how to make a living, at the same time. Thank you to Lamar Tyler, the millionaire hitmaker, for helping me to take my business to even higher heights and becoming unapologetic about being rich and Black. I'm forever grateful for your black-ity Blackness. A special shout-out to Randy, who has helped me problem-solve my way through many complex twists and turns on this entrepreneurship track, and to Toriano, who has taught me what it means to be genuinely free to do whatever you want to do.

My beloved literary angel and cheerleader, Benin Lemus, gets a big hug for combing through each word, and turning these pages over and over again, making sure I pour gallons of Black girl magic throughout this manuscript. Thank you for keeping me on my toes, meeting deadlines, and being the best hype woman a girl could ask for.

A big thank-you goes out to my editor, Sara Kendrick, for believing in me and giving me this unbelievable opportunity. You made this all possible. But I must give Linda Alila her flowers for the late-night editing sessions, for a listening ear to help pull the thoughts from my mind and place them eloquently between these pages. Thank you for your unwavering commitment to see me through to the finish line. To state that you're dope would be an understatement.

Ayyyeee for the A-Team, Alecia & Aundrea. Thank you to my sisters who believed in my vision that is The Stocks & Stilettos Society. A special thanks to Alecia for helping me live my best, bougie life while working tirelessly behind the scenes to keep this ship sailing. Many thanks to Aundrea for keeping it a buck by her no-nonsense and pragmatic style, while keeping me accountable to put my best foot forward to be the best boss chick

I was meant to be for the ladies that we serve. These ladies make me look good and have helped me take my message to the masses far beyond my wildest dreams.

This wouldn't be possible without all of my incredibly intelligent, smart, and beautiful StockSistars that help to make The Stocks & Stilettos Society a safe, yet fun space to learn about investing. Thank you for allowing me to be your fearless leader in this financial space.

Lastly, I want to thank my daughter and favorite human being for making sure not to let the money change me, that much. Your humor and old soul have pushed me through and I'm so honored that God chose me to be your mommy.

APPENDIX

Creating a dividend income strategy provides passive income for years to come. Use the Dividend Income Tracker below to help you put your own strategy in place. You can download this worksheet, access the dividend income calculator, and get the most up-to-date resources at http://fearlessfinances.com.

TICKER SYMBOL	EX-DIVIDEND DATE	CURRENT SHARE PRICE	DIVIDEND YIELD	NUMBER OF SHARES	QUARTERLY DIVIDEND	ANNUAL DIVIDEND INCOME

FEARLESS FIGURES

SAUNDRA DAVIS, MSFP, APFC, FBS,
https://sagefinancialsolutions.org

SHEENA ALLEN,
http://sheenaallen.com

ARNITA JOHNSON-HALL,
http://instagram.com/helloarnita

SYLVIA HALL

MAKEDA SMITH,
http://savvychicksinrealestate.com

GAIL PERRY-MASON,
http://instagram.com/gailpmason

ROBIN WATKINS,
http://meoaus.com

DAVONNE REAVES,
http://thevonnegroup.com

LISHA BELL,
http://blxvc.com

ENDNOTES

Introduction

1. Janice Traflet and Robert E. Wright, "America Doesn't Just Have a Gender Pay Gap. It Has a Gender Wealth Gap," *Washington Post,* April 2, 2019, https://www.washingtonpost.com/outlook/2019/04/02/america-doesnt-just-have-gender-pay-gap-it-has-gender-wealth-gap/.

Chapter 1

1. "Degrees Conferred by Race and Sex," Institute of Education Sciences, National Center for Education Statistics, 2020, https://nces.ed.gov/fastfacts/display.asp?id=72.
2. Carol S. Dweck, *Mindset: The New Psychology of Success* (New York: Ballantine Books, 2006).
3. Jonathan Edwards, "A Black Couple Says an Appraiser Lowballed Them. So, They 'Whitewashed' Their Home and Say the Value Shot Up," *Washington Post,* December 6, 2021, https://www.washingtonpost.com/nation/2021/12/06/black-couple-home-value-white-washing/; Jill Sheridan, "More Black Americans Call Out Housing Appraisal Process as Discriminatory," *NPR Morning Edition,* May 19, 2021, https://www.npr.org/2021/05/19/998137158/more-black-americans-call-out-housing-appraisal-process-as-discriminatory.
4. Freddie Mac, "Racial and Ethnic Valuation Gaps in Home Purchase Appraisals," September 20, 2021, http://www.freddiemac.com/research/insight/20210920_home_appraisals.page?.
5. Peter O'Dowd, "'The Whiteness of Wealth' Probes Why Black Americans Pay Higher Taxes," WBUR, May 17, 2021, https://www.wbur.org/hereandnow/2021/05/17/us-taxes-dorothy-brown.
6. Richard V. Reeves and Katherine Guyot, "Black Women Are Earning More College Degrees, but That Alone Won't Close Race Gaps." Brookings, December 4, 2017, https://www.brookings.edu/blog/social-mobility-memos/2017/12/04/black-women-are-earning-more-college-degrees-but-that-alone-wont-close-race-gaps/; "Degrees Conferred by Race and Sex": Sonia Thompson, "Despite Being the Most Educated, Black Women Earn Less Money at Work, in Entrepreneurship, and in Venture Capital. Here Are 3 Ways to Fix It." *Inc.,* August 22, 2019, https://www.inc.com/sonia-thompson/black-women-equal-pay-equity-how-to-make-progress.html.

7. Lorna Sabbian and Maddie Dychtwald, *Women and Financial Wellness: Beyond the Bottom Line*, 2018, https://www.ml.com/women-financial-wellness-age-wave.html.
8. Fidelity Investments, *2021 Women and Investing Study* (Smithfield, RI: FMR LLC, 2021), https://www.fidelity.com/bin-public/060_www_fidelity_com/documents/about-fidelity/FidelityInvestmentsWomen&InvestingStudy2021.pdf.

Chapter 2

1. *2017 FDIC National Survey of Unbanked and Underbanked Households*, Federal Deposit Insurance Corporation (Washington, DC: FDIC, 2017), https://economicinclusion.gov/downloads/2017_FDIC_Unbanked_HH_Survey_Report.pdf.
2. "Table A.3: Unbanked Rates by Household Characteristics," *FDIC National Survey of Unbanked and Underbanked Households: Appendix Tables*, Federal Deposit Insurance Corporation, https://www.fdic.gov/householdsurvey/2017/2017appendix.pdf; "Table A.4: Underbanked Rates by Household Characteristics," *FDIC National Survey of Unbanked and Underbanked Households: Appendix Tables*, Federal Deposit Insurance Corporation, https://www.fdic.gov/householdsurvey/2017/2017appendix.pdf.

Chapter 3

1. Ben Luthi, "What Is an Adverse Action Letter?" *Experian,* March 31, 2020. https://www.experian.com/blogs/ask-experian/what-is-an-adverse-action-letter/.

Chapter 4

1. "U.S. Bank Survey Says Women Are Leaving Money and Influence on the Table," US Bank, March 5, 2020, https://www.usbank.com/about-us-bank/company-blog/article-library/us-bank-survey-says-women-are-leaving-money-and-influence-on-the-table.html.
2. Fidelity Investments, *2021 Women and Investing Study* (Smithfield, RI: FMR LLC, 2021), https://www.fidelity.com/bin-public/060_www_fidelity_com/documents/about-fidelity/FidelityInvestmentsWomen&InvestingStudy2021.pdf .
3. Fidelity Investments, *2021 Women and Investing Study,* p. 3.
4. "Older Women and Poverty: Single & Minority Women," Women's Institute for a Secure Retirement (WISER), 2021, https://wiserwomen.org/fact-sheets/women-retirement-the-facts-and-statistics/older-women-and-poverty-single-minority-women/.
5. "Older Women and Poverty: Single & Minority Women."

6. Morgan Housel, "Here's the Most Overlooked Fact About How Warren Buffett Amassed His Fortune, Says Money Expert," CNBC, September 8, 2020, https://www.cnbc.com/2020/09/08/billionaire-warren-buffett -most-overlooked-fact-about-how-he-got-so-rich.html.

7. "S&P 500 Historical Annual Returns," Macrotrends, October 29, 2021, https://www.macrotrends.net/2526/sp-500-historical-annual-returns.

8. John, ESI Money, "I asked 100 Millionaires How They Spend, Save, and Invest, and They Told Me Exactly What I Expected to Hear," *Business Insider*, December 5, 2018, https://www.businessinsider.com/how -millionaires-manage-money-interviews-2018-12.

Chapter 5

1. "Accelerated Payment Calculator." Bankrate, https://www.bankrate .com/calculators/home-equity/additional-mortgage-payment -calculator.aspx.

2. Aly J. Yale, "Hiring a Real Estate Attorney: A Real Estate Investor's Guide," Million Acres, February 25, 2020, https://www.millionacres .com/real-estate-basics/hiring-real-estate-attorney-real-estate-investors -guide/.

Chapter 6

1. Tanza Loudenback, "The 3-Step Method to Get Wealthy and Stay That Way, According to a New Book on Money and Happiness," *Business In- sider*, January 25, 2021, https://www.businessinsider.com/personal -finance/staying-wealthy-requires-frugality-paranoia-2021-1

2. IRC Section 408(d)(2), https://www.law.cornell.edu/uscode/text /26/408.

3. "Step Transaction Doctrine," Wikipedia, https://en.wikipedia.org/wiki /Step_transaction_doctrine.

4. Julia Kagan, "Substantially Equal Periodic Payment (SEPP)," Investope- dia, November 20, 2020, https://www.investopedia.com/terms/s/sepp .asp

5. Internal Revenue Service, "Table 1. Taxpayers with Individual Retire- ment Arrangement (IRA) Plans, by Type of Plan, Tax Year 2018," Janu- ary 12, 2022, https://www.irs.gov/pub/irs-soi/18in01ira.xlsx.

6. Ruth Umoh, "Black Women Were Among the Fastest-Growing Entrepreneurs—Then Covid Arrived," *Forbes,* October 26, 2020. https:// www.forbes.com/sites/ruthumoh/2020/10/26/black-women-were -among-the-fastest-growing-entrepreneurs-then-covid-arrived/?sh =774043566e01.

7. Emma Hinchliffe, "The Number of Black Female Founders Who Have Raised More Than $1 Million Has Nearly Tripled Since 2018," *Fortune,*

December 2, 2020, https://fortune.com/2020/12/02/black-women
-female-founders-venture-capital-funding-vc-2020-project-diane/.

8. Kelly Anne Smith, "How to Retire Early with FIRE," *Forbes*, December
7, 2021, https://www.forbes.com/advisor/retirement/the-forbes-guide
-to-fire/.

Chapter 7

1. "Historical Performance of The Dividend Kings List," Dividend Growth
Investor, June 14, 2018, https://www.dividendgrowthinvestor.com/2018
/06/historical-performance-of-dividend.html.

2. John Divine, "2021's Dividend Aristocrats List: All 65 Stocks," *U.S. News
& World Report*, November 1, 2021. https://money.usnews.com/investing
/stock-market-news/articles/dividend-stocks-aristocrats.

3. "S&P 500 Dividend Aristocrats Methodology," S&P Dow Jones Indices, October 2021, https://www.spglobal.com/spdji/en/documents
/methodologies/methodology-sp-500-dividend-aristocrats.pdf.

4. Dilantha De Silva, "It Makes Sense for Berkshire Hathaway to Declare
a Dividend Later This Week, But It Might Not," Seeking Alpha, February 21, 2021, https://seekingalpha.com/article/4407778-makes-sense-for
-berkshire-hathaway-to-declare-dividend-later-this-week-might-not.

5. "Global X NASDAQ 100 Covered Call ETF (QYLD).," Yahoo! Finance,
2022, https://finance.yahoo.com/quote/QYLD?p=QYLD&.tsrc=fin-srch.

Chapter 8

1. https://www.zillow.com/research/october-2021-market-report-30299/.

2. https://www.zillow.com/home-values/.

3. https://www.zillow.com/san-francisco-ca/home-values/.

4. "Real Estate Investment Trust," Wikipedia, https://en.wikipedia.org
/wiki/Real_estate_investment_trust.

5. Daniel Goodwin, "Top 10 Reasons Real Estate Investors Are Jumping
into DSTs," Kiplinger, March 21, 2021, https://www.kiplinger.com
/real-estate/real-estate-investing/602456/top-10-reasons-real-estate
-investors-are-jumping-into-dsts.

6. Tyler Cauble, "Commercial Real Estate Syndication for Beginners," The
Cauble Group, February 22, 2021, https://www.tylercauble.com/blog
/commercial-real-estate-syndication-for-beginners.

Chapter 9

1. Financial Industry Regulatory Authority (FINRA),. "Crowdfunding and
the JOBS Act: What Investors Should Know," May 17, 2017, https://www
.finra.org/investors/alerts/crowdfunding-and-jobs-act.

Bonus Chapter

1. Janice Compton and Robert A. Pollak, "The Life Expectancy of Older Couples and Surviving Spouses," *PLOS One*, May 14, 2021, https://doi .org/10.1371/journal.pone.0250564.
2. https://www.fidelity.com/calculators-tools/all or https://www.msn .com/en-us/money/tools/savingscalculator.
3. Stacy Francis, "Op-ed: Recent Widows Need Financial Guidance After a Spouse's Death," CNBC, November 22, 2021, https://www.cnbc.com /2021/11/22/op-ed-recent-widows-need-financial-guidance-after-a -spouses-death.html.
4. "U.S. Marriage and Divorce Rates by State: 2009 & 2019," US Census Bureau, October 27, 2020, https://www.census.gov/library/visualizations /interactive/marriage-divorce-rates-by-state-2009-2019.html.
5. "Elder Justice Initiative: Elder Abuse and Elder Financial Exploitation Statutes," US Department of Justice, 2021, https://www.justice.gov /elderjustice/prosecutors/statutes.
6. Kim Parker and Eileen Patten, "The Sandwich Generation," The Pew Research Center, January 30, 2013, https://www.pewresearch.org /social-trends/2013/01/30/the-sandwich-generation/.

INDEX

ABOUT THE AUTHOR

As the founder and creator of The Stocks & Stilettos Society, CASSANDRA CUMMINGS is the fearless visionary, innovative entrepreneur, and stylish thought leader who has forged an unprecedented movement around women and investing. Cummings has become one of the most prominent figures in closing the gender investing gap of our time.

Cummings created The Stocks & Stilettos Society to bring a feminine touch to finances and, more specifically, investing. Building on this momentum, Cummings organically grew her community from the ground up on social media after she quickly learned she had a knack for delivering complicated concepts with easy-to-follow strategies. In just five years, the community has grown to be a one-stop, online hub for investment literacy and financial resources with a following of StockSistars across the entire socioeconomic spectrum.

Cummings is regularly featured in major publications including the *Wall Street Journal, Business Insider, Parenting* magazine, BuzzFeed, *Essence*, AfroTech, and *Black Enterprise.* Cassandra Cummings is a registered investment advisor (RIA) with a bachelor of science in accounting from the University of Southern California, and a certificate in women's entrepreneurship from Cornell University.

Learn more and download resources at
http://thefearlessfinances.com.